T0288390

CONCISE
LINCOLN
LIBRARY

—

EDITED BY RICHARD W. ETULAIN
AND SYLVIA FRANK RODRIGUE

WILLIAM C. HARRIS

Lincoln and Congress

Southern Illinois University Press
Carbondale

Southern Illinois University Press
www.siupress.com

The Concise Lincoln Library has been made possible
in part through a generous donation by the Leland E.
and LaRita R. Boren Trust.

Volumes in this series have been published with support from the Abraham Lincoln Bicentennial Founda-
tion, dedicated to perpetuating and expanding Lincoln's vision for America and completing America's
unfinished work.

Jacket illustration adapted from a painting by Wendy
Allen. All interior illustrations courtesy of the Library
of Congress, Washington, D.C.

Library of Congress Cataloging-in-Publication Data
Names: Harris, William C. (William Charles),
    1933– author.
Title: Lincoln and Congress / William C. Harris.
Description: Carbondale : Southern Illinois University
Press, 2017. | Series: Concise Lincoln library | Includes
bibliographical references and index.
Identifiers: LCCN 2016029961 | ISBN 9780809335718
(hardback) | ISBN 9780809335725 (ebook)
Subjects: LCSH: Lincoln, Abraham, 1809–1865—Rela-
tions with legislators. | United States. Congress—His-
tory—19th century. | United States—History—Civil
War, 1861–1865—Political aspects. | United States—
Politics and government—1861–1865. | BISAC: history
/ United States / Civil War Period (1850–1877). | his-
tory / United States / 19th Century. | political science
/ Government / Executive Branch. | political science
/ Government / Legislative Branch. | political science
/ Political Process / Leadership. | political science
/ Presidents & Heads of State.
Classification: LCC E459 .H294 2017 | DDC
973.7092—dc23 LC record available at https://lccn
.loc.gov/2016029961

Printed on recycled paper. ♻
This paper meets the requirements of ANSI/NISO
Z39.48-1992 (Permanence of Paper) ∞

To my descendants

May you always remember the contribution that Lincoln and

Congress made to saving the Union and ending slavery.

CONTENTS

Gallery of illustrations beginning on page 77

LINCOLN AND CONGRESS

INTRODUCTION

"By the constitution, the executive may recommend measures which he may think proper; and he may veto those he thinks improper; and it is supposed he may add to these, certain indirect influences to affect the action of congress. My political education" as a Henry Clay Whig "strongly inclines me against a very free use of any of these means, by the Executive, to control the legislation of the country. As a rule, I think it better that congress should originate, as well as perfect its measures, without external bias."[1] Abraham Lincoln wrote these words in a manuscript that he had prepared for delivery at Pittsburgh in February 1861 when he was en route to Washington to become president. Former Whigs, who were a majority in Lincoln's Republican Party, which controlled Congress after Southern members from the seceded states withdrew, had a similar "political education" and also subscribed to the doctrine of legislative supremacy in the government. After he assumed the presidency and the Civil War began, Lincoln's "rule" to follow his "political education" in his relations with Congress would be tested.

At first Lincoln's firm hand against the secessionists and his vigor in mobilizing the country in 1861 for the war received the hearty support of Republicans in Congress and also many Northern Democrats and border state Unionists. When the conflict became a horrific war with no apparent end in sight, Republicans as well as others began to question Lincoln's capacity for leadership in suppressing the rebellion. William Pitt Fessenden of Maine, who emerged as a leading

Republican in the Senate, wrote home on January 14, 1862, "We are in a world of trouble here. Everybody is grumbling because nothing is done. . . . If the President had his wife's *will* and would use it rightly, our affairs would look much better." Fessenden reported that he and his Republican friends in Congress had remained publicly silent in their criticism of Lincoln lest they discourage the people from supporting the war.[2]

By this time some Republican leaders, mainly those associated with the radical wing of the party, had concluded that only Congress could save the Union. On January 22, 1862, the radical representative Thaddeus Stevens announced, "If no other action were left to save the Republic from destruction, I believe we [Congress] have the power, under the Constitution, and according to its expressed provisions, to declare a dictator, without confining the choice to any officer of the Government." Although dismayed by events, and particularly Lincoln's failure to move against slavery, the Pennsylvania Republican expressed the hope that the necessity for a dictator would never arise. Like fellow radicals, a vociferous minority in the Republican Party, Stevens concluded that Congress had the right to abolish slavery and arm black men, a position that Lincoln refused to take until much later. Stevens argued that the seceded states had forfeited their constitutional authority over slavery by rebelling against the United States, and as a result, the federal government should act against it.[3]

In June 1862, Senator Charles Sumner of Massachusetts asserted that Congress by means of its legislative power should determine war policies. Sumner, who had emerged as a vocal radical spokesman in the Senate, boldly declared, "I claim for Congress all that belongs to any government in the exercise of the rights of war." The president, he said, "was only the instrument of Congress under the Constitution of the United States."[4] In the same year, Senator Lyman Trumbull of Illinois, the chairman of the Senate Judiciary Committee and erstwhile radical, was appalled by Connecticut Republican senator James Dixon's claim that the president had the power to appoint military governors in North Carolina and Tennessee without congressional approval. Trumbull exclaimed, "It is the most dangerous doctrine ever advocated under a Constitutional government. The president can command only according to the law that Congress prescribed. . . . He is just as much subject to our control as if we appointed him, except that we cannot remove him and substitute another in his place." In addition, Trumbull contended that "the whole doctrine of uncontrollable power in the President [was] dangerous to republican institutions."[5]

These pronouncements were probably more theoretical and rhetorical than a serious call for Congress to challenge the president's authority, even if the radicals and their supporters could obtain a majority in both chambers. Increasingly, however, other Republicans in Congress criticized Lincoln for his slowness in prosecuting the war; his appointment and retention of incompetent military commanders, notably General George B. McClellan; and his refusal to act quickly and forcibly against slavery. Later in the war, they also took issue with the president's lenient reconstruction policy. Their efforts culminated in the Wade-Davis bill in 1864, which Lincoln pocket vetoed. Senator Trumbull, who owed his senatorial election in 1855 to Lincoln, wrote to a friend in early 1864, "[You] would be surprised in talking with public men [in Congress] to find how few, when you come to get at their real sentiments, are for Mr. Lincoln's reelection. There is a distrust and fear that he is too undecided and inefficient to put down the rebellion."[6]

Thaddeus Stevens provided a similar opinion regarding the president's weak support in Congress when introducing a Pennsylvania editor and Lincoln supporter to Representative Isaac N. Arnold of Illinois. "Here is a man who wants to find a Lincoln member of Congress," Stevens told Arnold. "You are the only one I know, and I have come over [to your desk] to introduce my friend to you." Arnold, not to be outdone, declared, "Thank you. I know a good many such, and I will present your friend to them." Years later, Arnold thought that Stevens was more right than wrong about support for Lincoln in Congress after the first year of the war.[7]

Radical Republican anger against Lincoln sometimes boiled over. On the eve of the 1864 Republican National Convention, which would nominate a candidate for president, Massachusetts senator Henry Wilson made a virulent vocal attack on Lincoln at a White House reception, prompting a colleague to interrupt and inform the senator that the proper place to denounce the president, if he desired, was in the Senate. Wilson answered that he knew a public speech against the president would be a waste of time, since the people were for Lincoln and nothing could prevent his renomination.[8] In the end, after Lincoln's renomination, Wilson, Trumbull, Stevens, and other radicals in Congress reluctantly threw their support behind the president. The radicals insisted that they did so only to prevent the election of General McClellan and the Democrats, who were running on a peace platform that, if successful, would put the Union cause in jeopardy and, at least, permit slavery to continue under state control.

Despite concerns regarding Lincoln's leadership, the tensions created by the horrendous war, and lack of precedents to guide their efforts, the president and Congress actually worked better than might have been expected. Their success owed a great deal to Lincoln's Whig background, his moderate temperament, and the political realities that Republicans faced. Even congressional Democrats and border state conservatives often cooperated or went along with the president and his administration when the fundamental Union purpose of the war was at stake. All factions also often found common cause on legislation that did not directly involve the war, such as the Morrill Land-Grant College Act and the Pacific Railway Act, though both measures were weakly argued on grounds that they would aid the war effort, especially the completion of the railroad. Lincoln and the Republicans in Congress, whether radicals or conservatives (moderates in today's political lexicon), while differing on war powers, military commanders and strategy, constitutional issues, and the method and timing for ending slavery, agreed that reunion without compromise and eventually emancipation must be goals in the war. Both the president and the Republicans rallied around the party standard to accomplish these objectives in the war. Their achievements occurred despite disagreements, in which the president as well as Republicans in Congress bore some responsibility.

The scholarly debate over the relationship between Lincoln and Congress and the importance of each in formulating Civil War policies has been ongoing. Most historians have tended to exaggerate the significance of the Radical Republicans in this relationship. Civil War historian David Donald has warned, however, that though the radicals "were noisy and conspicuous, their historical importance has been overrated. [They] were only one of the many factions that pulled for control of the Lincoln administration."[9] Also, historian James A. Rawley has written that "too often, the evolution of legislation" in Congress has been seen not in the context of the exigencies of war, but as a "'Second American Revolution,' in which the capitalists, laborers, and farmers of the North and West drove from power in the National government the planting aristocracy of the South." He suggested that this was a false premise regarding Republican policies.[10]

Although Republicans like Senators Charles Sumner and Benjamin F. Wade and Congressman Thaddeus Stevens wanted to transform the South after the war, they did not have the support of Lincoln or the majority in Congress for truly radical political or economic measures. In fact, Republicans often clashed with each other over policies and procedures, which to some extent were influenced by personal differences. Senator Fessenden and his New England colleagues, for example, found it difficult to work with Senator Sumner and bitterly disliked the self-righteous and egotistical Massachusetts senator. Also, some congressional Republicans viewed Wade as a western bully.[11] (The western states are defined as nonslave states west of the Appalachian Mountains.) Despite their differences, Republicans in Congress, along with the War Democrats in the Union Party coalition, usually cooperated in the important legislative efforts to win the war, secure emancipation, and ensure Union control of the South. Like Lincoln and members of his administration, Republicans generally sought to preserve the principles and republican institutions of the first American Revolution, stopping short of the fabled second revolution claimed by some scholars and writers. These principles included constitutional liberties, which nonetheless were violated during the war, and also economic opportunity without artificial restraints on individuals.

Some Republicans, however, as early as 1862 advocated both a "hard war" against the rebels and a draconian settlement for the postwar South that would include the confiscation of property and emancipation. When pressed by Representative Charles A. Wickliffe of

Kentucky to state his opinion regarding the war's purpose, Stevens, the epitome of the Radical Republican, announced, "I am for subduing this rebellion, and I am for inflicting all the consequences of defeat on a fallen foe in an unjust war. I am for confiscating the property of the rebels, and making it pay the cost of this rebellion. Then I am for removing the cause [slavery]." In a follow-up question by Wickliffe as to whether the old Constitution should be restored, Stevens answered that it could be done only after restoring "all that has been stolen [and] all that has been expended in the war. Until full atonement and reparation is made, I shall never shake hands with the bloody murderers."[12] Later, Stevens demanded congressional approval of not only emancipation but also black civil liberties and voting rights.

Some expansion of the federal government necessarily occurred during the war. Yet neither the president nor Congress, as is often claimed, conspired to establish a permanently strong central government at the expense of the states and the provisions of the Constitution.[13] Government activity at all levels increased during the war to meet military and other needs, some of dubious legality (notably, the suppression of dissent). After the war, the federal system of government, despite the addition of the Fourteenth Amendment, continued in a robust fashion, and state and local authorities maintained their constituted prerogatives.

Lincoln, faithful to his "political education" as a Whig, never wanted to create a strong presidency. He announced in his last message to Congress on December 6, 1864, "The Executive power itself would be greatly diminished by the cessation of actual war." He promised that in restoring the Union largely as it had been, though without slavery, presidential "pardons and remissions of forfeitures [property?] would be [fairly] exercised."[14] Lincoln did not foresee a change in the powers of the government as established by the Founders, whom he revered. Furthermore, the majority in Congress, notwithstanding the passage of important legislation that would affect postwar America (for example, currency reform and the National Bank Act), agreed with Lincoln that the traditional federal system of government and the sanctity of republican institutions should be preserved, with little fundamental change. Some changes toward "modernization," as some historians have claimed, did occur as a result of wartime legislation, but these probably proved more gradual and natural for a growing nation than has been assumed and were not necessarily the result of congressional or federal action.

As president, Lincoln focused on policies and military strategies to win the war and restore the Union, which he perceived as clearly his responsibility and constitutional authority as commander in chief. He left other matters to Congress, though these might have an effect on the war. Lincoln relied on the War and Navy Departments, in conjunction with state officials, to work with the appropriate committees in Congress to secure legislation to raise the necessary forces and supply their needs. Nonetheless, he insisted on appointing the general officers and commanders in the army and the navy. With little input from the president, Secretary of the Treasury Salmon P. Chase hammered out the crucial financial policies with Thaddeus Stevens, chairman of the House of Representatives Ways and Means Committee, and William Pitt Fessenden, chairman of the Senate Finance Committee.

This book is an account of the partnership between Lincoln and Congress, which, while reflective of divisions in Congress and at times exhibiting tension and conflict between the two branches of the government, still came together to provide the collective leadership and means to win the Civil War, enact important legislation, and end slavery. It is hoped that the book will give the reader a better understanding of the difficulties that Lincoln and Congress faced in saving the Union, abolishing slavery, and providing for a brighter future for America.

SECESSION AND WAR

Even before he assumed the presidency on March 4, 1861, Lincoln found himself drawn into the debate in Congress over a proposed compromise designed to check the secession movement in the South. When the Thirty-Sixth Congress met on December 3, 1860, for its last session, it established a committee of thirteen members in the Senate and thirty-three in the House to recommend a solution to the crisis following the election of Lincoln in November.

Lincoln, who was still in Springfield, soon received disturbing reports from Republican friends in Washington, including Senator Lyman Trumbull, that pressure was increasing for Congress to compromise on the central feature of the Republican platform—no extension of slavery. Republicans did not yet constitute a majority in Congress and would do so only after congressmen from the secessionist states vacated their seats. Concerned that frightened and weak-kneed Republicans in Congress would join Democrats and border state Unionists to approve such a compromise, the president-elect angrily wrote to Trumbull, who agreed with him, on December 10 to demand that Republicans stand behind the party platform: "Let there be no compromise on the question of *extending* slavery. If there be, all our labor is lost, and, ere long, must be done again." On December 17, he again wrote the Illinois senator: "If any of our friends do prove false, and fix up a compromise on the territorial question, I am for fighting again—that is all." Nonetheless, he would agree to "an honest inforcement [*sic*] of the constitution—fugitive slave clause included."[1]

Lincoln's intervention had the desired effect on Republicans, with the notable exception of Senator William H. Seward. The New York senator had been defeated by the Illinois rail-splitter for the Republican nomination, and he was now considering Lincoln's offer as secretary of state. As a member of the Senate Committee of Thirteen, Seward had voted against the compromise package proposed by Senator John J. Crittenden of Kentucky and endorsed by Senator Stephen A. Douglas, which included a provision permitting the expansion of slavery in the territories. But on January 12, Seward took to the floor of the Senate and, in a sectional conciliatory speech, called for the approval of several provisions in the Crittenden Compromise. He proposed a constitutional amendment protecting slavery in the Southern states, the repeal of Northern personal liberty laws that prevented the return of fugitive slaves to their masters, and, by means of a complicated formula, a provision that would give slavery a chance in the Southwest.[2]

Northern Democrats and Southern Unionists applauded Seward's speech and another that followed on January 31. Even Lincoln, who was trying to persuade his recalcitrant rival to join the cabinet, at first professed to believe that Seward's compromise proposal did not violate his party's platform.[3] On the other hand, Republicans could hardly contain their anger toward Seward, who they believed had sacrificed the party's antislavery principles. William Pitt Fessenden, a rising leader in the Senate, restrained his public indignation against his fellow Republican and chose not to reply to Seward in a speech. Instead, he wrote to a family member, "The ultra South will accept nothing which can be conceded, and the Democracy of the North [is] doing all it can to encourage disunion for the purpose of disgracing us." Fessenden indicated that the shameful actions of their opponents and Seward had united the Republicans against any compromise. "The country cannot be saved," he concluded, "by acknowledging that its government has no power to protect itself." The Maine senator believed, "Mr. Lincoln will be peacefully inaugurated, and then everything will depend upon his wisdom and tact."[4]

Even Frances Seward admonished her husband for conceding too much to the secessionists. She wrote him that the "compromises" in his speeches placed him "in danger of taking the path which led

Daniel Webster to an unhonored grave ten years ago" for his support of the Compromise of 1850.[5] The New Yorker's ill-fated position
caused Republicans in Congress, who would soon be in the majority,
to have serious doubts that Seward could be trusted. Anti-Seward
sentiment grew after he became secretary of state and sought to
dominate the Lincoln administration.

The Crittenden Compromise seemed dead in February when
its supporters in the House of Representatives failed to secure the
suspension of the two-thirds rule for the proposal's consideration.
However, in late February, a meeting of a "Peace Conference" called
by the border slave states recommended concessions to the South in
order to save the Union. It gained the support of some Republicans
in Congress and provided Senator Crittenden, along with his followers, renewed hope that his compromise could still be enacted.[6]

Disturbed by the prospect that the compromise might pass on the
eve of Congress's adjournment and Lincoln's inauguration, Trumbull
on March 2 spoke forcibly against it in the Senate. He placed the
onus for the crisis squarely on the Southern secessionists, not on the
Republicans as many Northern Democrats, including incumbent
president James Buchanan, and border state sponsors of the compromise had done. Trumbull even turned his rhetorical guns on
the venerable Senator Crittenden. Although he did not question the
Kentucky senator's loyalty, Trumbull said that instead of denouncing
"those who violate the Constitution and trample the flag of the country in the dust," Crittenden "talks to us of [Republican] usurpations,
of our dogmas; tells us that for a straw we are willing to dissolve the
Union and involve the country in blood." The Illinois senator announced that if Crittenden "employed some of [his] eloquence . . .
in defense of the Constitution as it is, and in favor of maintaining
the laws and Government, we should see a very different state of
things in the country."[7]

Trumbull, whose views coincided with those of Fessenden and
other Republican leaders in Congress, insisted that the "remedy for
the existing difficulties [is] to clothe the Government with sufficient
power to maintain itself." He assured finicky members of Congress,
"when that is done, and you have an Executive with the disposition

to maintain the authority of the Government," which he expected with Lincoln, "[no] gun need be fired to stop the further spread of secession." When Southerners see that the new administration "is resolved to maintain its authority, and, at the same time, to make no encroachments whatever upon [their] rights, the desire to secede will subside." Trumbull in his March 2 speech predicted that after a year of the Republican government, Southerners would realize that "they are just as safe in all their rights, just as little interfered with in regard to their domestic institutions, as under any former Administration. [Then] they will have no disposition to inaugurate civil war and commence an attack upon the Federal Government."[8]

Two days later, on inauguration day, Congress rejected all but one of the Peace Conference's compromise provisions, notably a proposed constitutional amendment prohibiting federal interference with slavery in the states. Lincoln and some Republican members of Congress did not seriously object to it, since they believed that the proposed amendment was redundant; they had always denied the right of the federal government to interfere with the "peculiar institution" in the South. Two weeks after its initiation by Congress, the new president dutifully sent the proposed amendment to the states for their action. If approved, it would have become the Thirteenth Amendment to the Constitution. The onslaught of war and the growing Northern resistance to any concession to the South forestalled the states' ratification of the amendment.[9]

Realistically, no compromise would have persuaded the lower South to return to the Union, though at least for a time it would have quelled secessionist sentiment in the upper South. When Lincoln took the oath of office as president, the issue had become the military coercion of the seceded states or, more immediately, the status of the federal forts and installations in these states. Lincoln in his inaugural address attempted in vain to reassure his "disaffected fellow countrymen" that he would respect all their rights.[10] But his declaration that it was his constitutional duty to enforce federal laws (which were few) and protect U.S. property in the South strongly suggested that armed conflict was virtually inevitable.

Although the Thirty-Sixth Congress ended the day before the inauguration, the new Senate convened immediately and briefly to act on the new president's appointments to office. Now dominated by Republicans, the Senate without opposition from the demoralized Democratic minority selected its committee chairmen and members to serve during the brief session. The Senate approved Lincoln's list of appointments, which the president had been slow in providing. Senator Fessenden, however, privately revealed his concern that Lincoln, whom he publicly praised, had neglected New England's claims to office in favor of westerners. Fessenden also "was pained and disgusted with the ill-bred, ravenous crowd" of westerners who flooded the White House after the inauguration, reminiscent of when Andrew Jackson became president.[11]

Before the Senate adjourned in late March, a vigorous debate over the meaning of Lincoln's inaugural address broke out between Republicans and upper South Democrats whose states had not seceded. Senator Thomas L. Clingman of North Carolina on the second day of the special session declared that the president's address was a war message. Senator Douglas, in what turned out to be his swan song in the Senate (he died on June 3), reminded Clingman as well as others that the president had pledged his administration "to a peaceful solution of our national difficulties." Furthermore, Douglas pointed out, on the sensitive issue of slavery, Lincoln was "explicit and certain upon the point that [he] will not directly or indirectly interfere" with the institution within the states. The Illinois Democrat also implied that the president would defer to Congress on the enforcement of future federal laws in the seceded states.

On March 28, the last day of the special Senate session, Senator Trumbull offered a resolution supporting a policy of federal coercion if necessary to maintain the Union: "*Resolved*, That . . . the true way to preserve the Union is to enforce the laws of the Union; that resistance to their enforcement, whether under the name of anti-coercion or any other name, is encouragement to disunion; and that it is the duty of the President to use all the means in his power to hold and protect the public property of the United States, and enforce the laws thereof" in the seceded states as well as in the other states.[12] Although

Trumbull did not ask for a Senate vote on the resolution, it clearly expressed the sentiment of Republicans in Congress who had gone home to await developments in the crisis. Trumbull's resolution and his party's overwhelming support for it must also have strengthened President Lincoln's resolve, as stated in his inaugural address, to protect federal property (installations and forts) in the wayward states.

Two weeks after the special session of the Senate adjourned, the president dispatched a relief expedition to sustain Fort Sumter in Charleston Harbor. On April 12, the Confederate guns around the harbor opened fire on the uncompleted fort, followed by the federal garrison's surrender. With the unanimous support of his advisors, including Senator Douglas, who was still in Washington, Lincoln on April 15 issued a fateful proclamation calling for 75,000 militiamen to suppress the insurrection in the South "and to cause the laws to be duly executed." At the same time, the president, "deeming that the present condition of public affairs presents an extraordinary occasion," summoned the new Congress to convene on July 4 "to consider and determine, such measures, as in their wisdom, the public safety, and interest may seem to demand."[13] The July 4 date for the Thirty-Seventh Congress to assemble obviously had symbolic, patriotic value. The eleven-week interval from the president's call on April 15 to Congress's convening also would provide time for members from the distant West to travel to Washington. The delay, contrary to what often has been assumed, was not because Lincoln wanted a period of freedom in which to act without congressional complications, but rather to give members sufficient time to arrive in the capital, permit elections to Congress to take place in several states, and allow Lincoln to write a report on his actions.

After issuing his April 15 proclamation, Lincoln moved quickly to prepare for what he fervently hoped would be a brief war, and with the limited Union purpose that he had set forth in the document. On April 19, he proclaimed a naval blockade of the insurrectionary states, which, however, could not possibly become effective immediately. In fact, it never became airtight. When rioting against Massachusetts troops passing through Baltimore erupted and the national capital came under virtual siege by secessionists, the president on April 27 suspended the writ of habeas corpus along the Washington-Philadelphia corridor. With the upper South moving to join the Confederate states, Lincoln soon realized that the seventy-five thousand militiamen in his call would be inadequate to suppress the rebellion. On May 3, he issued a call for 42,034 volunteers and also ordered an increase in the small regular army and navy. He promised to submit both actions to Congress for authorization when it met.[14]

The wartime political and social atmosphere in Washington when the Thirty-Seventh Congress assembled on July 4, 1861, did not provide for calm deliberations by the lawmakers. Yet much was accomplished. In the White House, Lincoln must have been greatly distracted by the sounds and scenes on the streets, as well as the importunities for positions and favors. Thousands of troops flooded into the capital, where hundreds of Southern residents either supported the secessionists or opposed the war, adding to the confusion and tension in the streets. Military bands blared, officers and sergeants barked orders, and army wagons clattered up and down Pennsylvania and other avenues. Tipsy and drunken soldiers could be seen and heard on the streets, often culminating in fights.[15] Even some congressmen succumbed to the bottle before the end of the session in early August. Senator Orville H. Browning of Illinois, who had replaced the deceased "Little Giant," disgustedly recorded in his diary on August 5, "Several of the Senators were quite drunk to day, especially [James A.] McDougall [of California] & [Willard] Saulsbury [of Delaware], and some scenes were enacted which ought not to occur in a body occupying so exalted & dignified a position as the Senate of the U.S."[16]

Already, by the summer, civilian contractors and hangers-on were busy seeking the main chance in the national capital. Prostitutes inevitably had followed the troops into town and were plying their trade. A western officer reported distastefully, "Hoops and buttons have the highways and byways, ogling each other." He further wrote, "Beauty and sin done up in silk, with the accompaniment of lustrous eyes and luxurious hair, on every thoroughfare offer themselves for [money]."[17]

Despite the temptations and feverish activity on the streets and on Capitol Hill, Congress worked with zeal to satisfy the president's needs for conducting the war. Republicans or supporters of the Union Party coalition had a solid majority in both houses and, though divided on some issues and often on parliamentary procedures, were clearly able to control the new Congress. Their party caucuses quickly settled on the committee memberships. Because of their seniority, energy, and perhaps intellect, New England Republicans dominated the important Senate committees and to a lesser extent those in the House of Representatives. For example, William Pitt Fessenden became chairman of the Senate Finance Committee; Charles Sumner, the Foreign Relations Committee; and Henry Wilson of Massachusetts, the Military Affairs Committee. The venerable Solomon Foot of Vermont served as president pro tempore of the Senate (there was no Senate majority leader during the nineteenth century). Vice President Hannibal Hamlin of Maine presided over the Senate. Foot's equally distinguished Vermont colleague Jacob Collamer served as an important moderating influence in Congress. Lyman Trumbull of Illinois, a native of Connecticut who had lived for four years in Georgia, broke the New England monopoly on Senate leadership when he was chosen to chair the Judiciary Committee. In December 1861, Benjamin F. Wade of Ohio, who had been raised in western Massachusetts, became chairman of the powerful and controversial Joint Committee on the Conduct of the War created by Congress. Wade also headed the Senate Committee on Territories, an important committee in the nineteenth century.

The New England influence was not as significant in the House of Representatives. Thaddeus Stevens of Pennsylvania at age sixty-nine was chosen chairman of the Ways and Means Committee, the most important committee in the lower chamber. After a heated contest, Galusha A. Grow, also of the Keystone State, became Speaker of the House. His main rival was Francis "Frank" P. Blair Jr., of Missouri, the scion of the prominent Blair family of Maryland; his brother Montgomery was Lincoln's postmaster general. Frank Blair, a man of strong passions and prejudices whom Lincoln liked nonetheless, never got over his defeat as speaker. By the end of the war, he had become a Democrat and served as a general in William Tecumseh Sherman's army. Other leading Republicans in the House were young Schuyler Colfax of Indiana, a rising star in the party; Elihu Washburne of Illinois, a friend of Lincoln's; Elbridge G. Spaulding of New York; Henry L. Dawes of Massachusetts; John A. Bingham of Ohio, who chaired the Committee on the Judiciary; and Justin S. Morrill of Vermont.[18]

Except perhaps for Stevens and Sumner, it is impossible to accurately categorize any of the Republican members of Congress as true radicals at the beginning of the war. Some Republicans became more radical on war issues and slavery as time went by and the conflict grew increasingly destructive. Others, such as Senators Trumbull and Fessenden, moved back and forth between radical and middle-of-the-road positions, depending on the issue's significance to the war and political concerns at home. Even Stevens and Sumner occasionally voted with the Democrats on procedural questions. With some exceptions, such as Stevens and Wade, lower North members tended to be more conservative than those of the upper North. Republican support for Lincoln also was usually stronger in the lower Northern states, where members of the party faced serious Democratic challenges and realized the importance of moderating their positions and rhetoric.

Relatively large Democratic delegations from the key states of New York and the lower North, along with border state Unionists, provided a spirited challenge in the House to Republican proposals that they determined were radical. The delegations included John J. Crittenden, the aging former senator of Kentucky, who had returned to Congress in July 1861 as a member of the House and was an influential voice for the loyal opposition until his death in 1863. Clement Vallandigham of Ohio emerged as the most vocal Democrat in the Thirty-Seventh Congress; by late 1862, he had become the leader of the Peace Democrats, or Copperhead faction of the party.

Although supportive of the war, the Democrats and border state Unionists, after a brief honeymoon period with Lincoln during the first months of the war, pulled few punches in criticizing the president, the conduct of the war, military arrests, Republican confiscation of property, antislavery policies, the recruitment of black troops, and military conscription. Yet on some important issues, such as the land-grant college bill, Pacific railway bill, homestead bill, and currency legislation, they often were divided. In the Senate, the Democrats and border state senators were at times joined in their votes by conservative Republicans James R. Doolittle of Wisconsin, Orville H. Browning of Illinois, Edgar Cowan of Pennsylvania, and James Dixon of Connecticut.

On July 5, the day after they assembled, members of Congress listened as a clerk read one of the most important messages Abraham Lincoln ever wrote. The president began by explaining the actions that he had taken since becoming president. He said that he had acted to fulfill his inaugural address promise "only to hold the public places and property, not already wrested from the Government, and to collect the revenue; relying for the rest, on time, discussion, and the ballot-box." As he told Congress, he had given "repeated pledges against any disturbance to any of the people, or any of their rights," and he "looked to the exhaustion of all peaceful measures, before a resort to any stronger ones" became necessary. When faced with the surrender of Fort Sumter, Lincoln indicated that to abandon it, "under the circumstances, would be utterly ruinous. [It] would discourage the friends of the Union, embolden its adversaries, and go far to insure the latter, a recognition abroad—that, in fact, it would be our national destruction consummated. This could not be allowed."[19]

The president went on to explain why Fort Pickens in Pensacola Harbor, despite his hopes, could not be reinforced as a symbol of Union control "before a crisis would be reached at Fort Sumter." He therefore acted to resupply Fort Sumter; at the same time, he "expressly notified" the authorities in Charleston that "the garrison in the fort" was there "not to assail them, but merely to maintain visible possession, and thus to preserve the Union from actual, and immediate dissolution." But the South Carolina forces chose to attack and reduce the fort, he said. "In this act, discarding all else," Lincoln announced, "they have forced upon the country, the distinct issue: 'Immediate dissolution, or blood.'"[20]

"This issue," he wrote, "embraces more than the fate of these United States. It presents to the whole family of man, the question, whether a constitutional republic, or a democracy—a government of the people, by the same people—can, or cannot, maintain its territorial integrity, against its own domestic foes." The test had come on the issue, he said, and "no choice was left" for him but to resist the destruction of the republic by "call[ing] out the war power of the Government." He immediately called for troops from the states, whose response, Lincoln reported, "was most gratifying, surpassing, in unanimity and spirit, the most sanguine expectation," except for the border slave states of Maryland, Kentucky, and Missouri, which attempted to remain neutral. The measures he had taken, Lincoln told Congress, "whether strictly legal or not, were ventured upon, under what appeared to be a popular demand, and a public necessity; trusting then as now, that Congress would readily ratify them. It is believed that nothing has been done beyond the constitutional competency of Congress."[21]

The president reported to Congress his reason for authorizing the suspension of the writ of habeas corpus between Washington and Philadelphia. Although admitting that "the legality and propriety" of his decision had been questioned, Lincoln wrote that he had acted because "the whole of the laws which were required to be faithfully executed, were being resisted, and failing of execution, in nearly one-third of the States." He asked, "Must they be allowed to finally fail of execution [by] some single law, made in such extreme tenderness of the citizen's liberty, that practically, it relieves more of the guilty, than of the innocent, should, to a very limited extent, be violated?" Lincoln famously declared, "To state the question more directly, are all the laws, *but one*, to go unexecuted, and the government itself go to pieces, lest that one be violated?" However, he did not think that his suspension of the writ had violated the law, since, he claimed, the Constitution was silent on which branch of the government could exercise the power in "a dangerous emergency." He could not believe that "the framers of the instrument intended, that in every case, the danger," alluding to the rebellion, should be permitted to "run its course, until Congress could be called together." He left it "entirely to the better judgment of Congress" whether any further action should be taken on the suspension of the writ of habeas corpus.[22]

Much of the president's July 4 address to Congress described the flaws in Southern secession and why it was unconstitutional. Lincoln even charged that the secession movement was a conspiracy of a minority that "commenced by an insidious debauching of the public mind" to incite rebellion, "until, at length, they [had] brought many good men to a willingness to take up arms against the government the day *after* some assemblage of men [had] enacted the farcical pretense of taking their State out of the Union." The Union, Lincoln declared, was "older than any of the States; and, in fact, it created them as States," and they could not legally break away from the Union. Yet he admitted that "unquestionably the States have the powers, and rights, reserved to them in, and by the National Constitution."[23]

Except for a few Democrats and border state men, members of Congress praised the president's July 4 message. Senator Browning expressed the sentiment of Republican colleagues when he noted in his diary that the message was "a most admirable history of our present difficulties, and a conclusive and unanswerable argument against the abominable heresy of secession."[24] The president's message, which he took great pains in drafting, unfortunately has often received only brief attention by historians, perhaps because of its length (more than six thousand words) and because it failed to meet the grandeur of the Gettysburg Address and the Second Inaugural Address. However, Lincoln scholar James G. Randall, writing in the 1940s, concluded that the message "stands as one of the most elaborate and carefully prepared papers" of any president. It superbly "comprised a history of events, a report of stewardship, a constitutional argument, and an exalted commentary of fundamentals."[25] Modern Lincoln scholar Douglas L. Wilson similarly writes, "While not one of the most famous or most familiar of Lincoln's presidential writings, the July 4 message to Congress was nonetheless one of his most important in establishing his stature as a stand-up leader and a man to be reckoned with." It also exemplified "Lincoln's confidence in his own ability to accomplish important ends through writing."[26]

In addition to reporting on the actions he had taken, the president asked Congress to give him "the legal means for making this contest a short, and a decisive one." He recommended that Congress "place at the control of the government, for the work, at least four hundred thousand men, and four hundred millions of dollars." The debt to be accrued, Lincoln calculated, would be "less sum per head" in dollar value "than was the debt of our revolution." He predicted, "A right result, at this time, will be worth more to the world, than ten times the men, and ten times the money" that will be needed to suppress the insurrection. "Surely," Lincoln told Congress, "each man has as strong a motive *now*, to *preserve* our liberties, as each had" in the Revolution "to *establish* them."[27]

On July 10, a joint resolution was introduced to endorse all actions that Lincoln had taken, including the suspension of the writ of habeas corpus along the Eastern Corridor. Inspired by the president's message, public demand, and patriotic fervor, Republicans and even many Democrats joined in urging quick congressional support for the president's actions, as well as approval of his recommendations.[28] Some Democrats and border state members, however, had strong reservations about giving the president carte blanche over the use of the troops and how the money would be spent. For example, in the House, Samuel S. "Sunset" Cox, Democratic representative of an Ohio district that bordered on the slave South, announced, "I will vote for what is required to enable the Executive to sustain the Government—not to subjugate the South, but to vindicate the honor, peace, and power of the Government."[29]

The House of Representatives rejected the Democratic concerns and on July 15, by an overwhelming majority, approved the joint resolution endorsing Lincoln's actions. Only five representatives voted against it, two from Kentucky and three from the North.[30] One opposing voter was Henry C. Burnett, who would soon preside over a meeting creating Kentucky's provisional Confederate government; he later served as a Confederate senator. Another opponent of the resolution was Benjamin Wood, whose brother Fernando Wood would become New York's most notorious Copperhead. Some Democrats chose not to vote on the resolution.

In the Senate, the debate became volatile when John C. Breckinridge, the day after the House vote, leveled his rhetorical guns against the joint resolution, and particularly President Lincoln. The former vice president and Southern rights Democratic presidential candidate, who, like Burnett, would cast his lot with the Confederacy, thundered that if the resolution passed, the Senate would put "in the hands of the President of the United States the power of a dictator." The president, he declared, had already acted on the doctrine of necessity to preserve the Union, a position that "[was] utterly subversive of all written limitations of government." The president, the Kentucky senator predicted, would feel warranted "to subordinate the civil to the military, suspend the writ [of habeas corpus], declare martial law, and suppress the press," all of which would be justified under the doctrine of necessity. Although Breckinridge admitted that emancipation at this time was "no object contemplated for which the war [was] to be prosecuted," he claimed that the Lincoln administration "may, in their madness and folly and treason, make the abolition of slavery one of the results of this war. That is what I understand [wrongly] to be precisely the position of the Administration upon the subject of this war."[31] Breckinridge's long speech was interrupted several times by a raucous pro-Southern gallery that shouted its approval.

Although some Republican senators, as well as others, had concerns regarding the extraordinary authority granted the president, the Senate, along with the House, overwhelmingly approved the resolution giving Lincoln what he wanted—and more—to support the war. The president had asked for 400,000 troops. Congress, shocked by the army's defeat on July 21 at Bull Run in Virginia, authorized him to raise 500,000 men, which included the 230,000 men that had already been enlisted for three years.[32] Secretary of the Treasury Chase, House Ways and Means Committee chairman Stevens, and Senate Finance Committee chairman Fessenden worked out the federal loan and taxing provisions. Chase estimated that $320 million would be needed during the first year of the war alone. Congress approved $80 million in taxes, including direct taxes that would be apportioned among the states and a federal income tax, the first in American history. Congress also authorized the administration to borrow approximately $333 million in Treasury notes, an amount exceeding what Chase had requested. Western members of Congress in both parties, however, grumbled that the taxes would fall too heavily on the farmers of their section, while the banking, manufacturing, and commercial properties of the Northeast would not suffer. As it turned out, the loan legislation also benefited the Northeast at the expense of the West. In one of the closest votes of the summer session, the financial package passed by 77 to 60 in the House and 34 to 8 in the Senate, with several prominent western Republicans opposing it, including some who would be identified with the radical wing of the party.[33]

Meanwhile, in an action that would have important consequences for reconstruction, the Senate seated John S. Carlile and Waitman T. Willey of the Restored (Union) Government of Virginia, whose formation Lincoln had encouraged. In addition, the House of Representatives dutifully satisfied the president by seating three western Virginia claimants. Both Carlile and Willey were small slaveholders of western Virginia. Carlile became a conservative activist in the Senate, while Willey, though proslavery in 1861, eventually affiliated with the Republicans. The Restored Government of Virginia, which survived the war, provided the constitutional means for the creation of the state of West Virginia in 1863.[34] Republicans in Congress, especially radicals like senators Ben Wade and Charles Sumner, would rue the day that they agreed to the Virginia precedent for the president's reconstruction initiative.

One congressional measure Lincoln did not want was a confiscation bill that Congress hammered out over a two-week period late in the summer session. On July 15, Lyman Trumbull of Illinois and Zachariah Chandler of Michigan introduced separate bills in the Senate "to confiscate property used for insurrectionary purposes." The bills were referred to the Judiciary Committee, which Trumbull chaired.[35] The committee, however, divided on the issue of confiscation, whereupon Trumbull, inflamed by reports that the Confederates had used "slaves as a component element" of their army in the Battle of Bull Run, introduced a personal confiscation bill that included slave property. After a brief debate, the bill passed the Senate by a 33 to 6 vote, with the border state senators, as expected, opposing it.[36]

When the confiscation bill went to the House, former senator John J. Crittenden spoke out against it, reminding his colleagues that Congress had no power, whether during wartime or peacetime, to legislate regarding slavery in the states. Furthermore, Crittenden pointed out that the Constitution prohibited the forfeiture of property beyond the lifetime of the owner, which the bill did not prohibit.[37] Although Stevens and other radicals listened respectfully to the aging Crittenden, the Republican leadership agreed that the confiscation of slaves would apply only to those who were used for rebel military purposes. The bill did not guarantee freedom for the confiscated slaves. The House passed the measure by a vote of 60 to 48, with seven Republicans joining Democrats and border state members in opposition.[38]

Lincoln, though opposed to the principle of confiscation without the owner having an opportunity for judicial redress, signed the bill. He believed that it would create more harm than good in that it would cause the rebels to fight harder and would hurt the Union cause in the border states. But Lincoln concluded, according to Republican James G. Blaine, that "he could not however veto the bill, because that would be equivalent to declaring that the Confederate army might have the full benefit of the slave population as a military force."[39]

Most members in 1861 wanted Congress to state clearly, in the form of a resolution by each chamber, the purpose of the war. They believed that such a statement should be compatible with Lincoln's declaration of the limited Union objective in the conflict. It should be designed to placate sentiment not only in the critical border slave states but also among Northerners who opposed emancipation and the "subjugation" of the Southern people.

With this purpose in mind, on July 22 Crittenden introduced in the House a resolution that he had announced earlier. The resolution declared "that the present deplorable civil war has been forced upon the country by the disunionists of the Southern States now in revolt against the Constitutional Government; . . . that this war is not waged upon our part in any spirit of oppression, nor for any purpose of conquest or subjugation, nor purpose of overthrowing or interfering with the rights or established institutions of those States, but to defend and maintain the supremacy of the Constitution and preserve the Union, with all the dignity, equality, and rights of the several States unimpaired; and that as soon as these objects are accomplished the war ought to cease."[40] The Crittenden Resolution passed by a surprisingly large vote of 117 to 2. Stevens and a handful of antislavery radicals, despite a desire for a statement calling for the subjugation of the South, voted for the Crittenden Resolution.[41]

In the Senate, Andrew Johnson of Tennessee, the only senator from a secessionist state, offered an identical resolution on July 25. A debate immediately broke out over some of the wording in the resolution, mainly the meaning of "subjugation." Trumbull wanted an unequivocal statement "that this war is prosecuted for the purpose of subjugating all rebels and traitors who are in arms against the Government." He denied criticism that he "proposed to subjugate States" or the Union people in the South. Senator Jacob Collamer of Vermont played down the meaning of the word "subjugation," pointing out that it "was frequently used in political practice as a sort-of catch-word" and did not really mean the suppression of a people, in this case the Southern people. Conservative Republican senator James Doolittle reminded his colleagues that the purpose of the war was strictly to maintain the Constitution and the laws under it, and "to preserve the Union with the rights and dignity of the States all unimpaired."[42]

Speaking for Virginia Unionists, Waitman T. Willey, fresh from taking his seat as a senator of the state's rump Union government, strongly backed the Johnson Resolution. He predicted that its passage "will give muscle and vigor to every loyal arm in the Old Dominion." Willey, however, warned, "If it should ever be intimated or declared that this is to be a war upon the domestic institutions of the South, and upon the rights of private property, every loyal arm on the soil of the Old Dominion will be instantly paralyzed."[43]

William Pitt Fessenden made the most telling statement by a Republican in support of the Johnson Resolution. He announced, "I do not want to carry on this war for the purpose of subjugating the people of any State in any shape or form, and it is a false idea gotten up by bad men for bad purposes that it has ever been the purpose of any portion of the people of this country." But, Fessenden insisted, the Union people of the North "have a purpose . . . to defend the

Constitution and the laws of the country, and to put down this revolt at any hazard; and it is for them to say whether it is necessary for us in the course of accomplishing a legitimate and proper object to subjugate [the rebels] in order to do it." The Maine senator, however, said that he would not "want to keep them subjugated [any] longer than was necessary to secure that purpose."[44]

Fessenden's support for the Johnson Resolution brought in line uncertain Republicans, and on July 25 it passed the Senate by a vote of 30 to 5, but with several senators absent.[45] Four border state Democrats opposed the resolution because it condemned "the disunionists" of the South for causing the war but not the Republicans of the North. Three of the dissenting senators—Breckinridge, Trusten Polk, and Waldo P. Johnson—soon joined the Confederacy; they were replaced by former Whigs. A fourth Democrat, Lazarus W. Powell, remained in the Senate and became a thorn in the side of Lincoln and the Republicans on issues relating to slavery, constitutional liberties, and states' rights. Trumbull voted against the Johnson Resolution because it did not go far enough in calling for the punishment of the rebels.

Congress adjourned on August 6, to reconvene at its regular time in December. Lincoln must have been pleased with the work of the summer session of Congress, since it approved all his actions and also provided him with the necessary means to fight the war. Furthermore, Congress had passed the Crittenden-Johnson Resolutions, which endorsed the conservative purpose in the war, the same that Lincoln had proclaimed at the beginning of the conflict. The resolutions had received a near unanimous vote in Congress, which included Democrats and most border state Unionists. Such an overwhelming vote would not have occurred if an antislavery statement and harsh penalties on the South had been included, as some Republicans such as Thaddeus Stevens desired. For the time being, Stevens radicals agreed to support the limited, fundamental objective in the war—the restoration of the Union.

Lincoln soon realized that underneath the support for the Union-only aim in the war simmered a sentiment among some members of his own party to add emancipation and the confiscation of Southern property as Union objectives in the conflict. That view became apparent in late August and early September, when General John C. Frémont ordered, without consulting the president, the confiscation of rebel property, including slaves, in Missouri and parts of Kentucky, areas under his command. When the general refused Lincoln's request to rescind the order pertaining to the slaves, the president, faced with the immediate possibility of losing Kentucky, revoked it.

Lincoln's revocation of Frémont's antislavery order provoked a storm of protest among antislavery Protestant leaders in the North as well as Republicans, including some who were hardly antislavery stalwarts, such as Senator Browning. Lincoln's Illinois friend informed the president that Frémont's order conformed to the recently enacted Confiscation Act. (It actually exceeded the law.) Browning also said that the order conformed to the "universal acknowledged principles of international political law" in warfare regarding the seizure of rebel property.[46] The president, however, stood by his decision. At home in New England, and before the revocation of the order, Senator Fessenden wrote to a friend with some exaggeration, "You have no idea of the electric effect" of Frémont's proclamation "upon all parts of the country. Men feel now as if there was something tangible and real in this contest." When Lincoln removed Frémont from command in early November, Fessenden denounced his action as "cruel" and "inexcusable," saying that because of his action, "the President has lost ground amazingly." The Maine senator charged that Lincoln's removal of General Frémont, who was "showing great qualities as a soldier" and a statesman, "was a weak and unjustifiable concession to the Union men of the border States."[47] Few historians would agree with Fessenden's opinion of Frémont's sterling qualities.

Upset with the president's failure to support General Frémont, Radical Republicans such as Senator Sumner and Congressmen Stevens, James Eliot of Massachusetts, and Owen Lovejoy of Illinois were determined to make emancipation an objective in the war when Congress assembled in December. The disaster of a Union force at Ball's Bluff, Virginia, on October 21, 1861, in which Oregon senator and colonel Edward D. Baker was killed, added to Republican frustration and contributed to the growing belief that Lincoln did not understand the nature of the war and thus was unequal to the task of managing it.

On November 5, Senator Trumbull expressed the dismay of many Republican colleagues when he wrote to a friend, "In my opinion this rebellion ought to have and might have been crushed before this." The president "means well and in ordinary times would have made one of the best of Presidents, but he lacks confidence in himself and the *will* necessary in this great emergency." Trumbull complained "that there is still remaining an influence" in the administration "[that is] almost if not quite controlling, which I fear is looking more to some grand diplomatic move for the settlement of our troubles than to the strengthening of our arms. It is only by making this war terrible to traitors that our difficulties can be permanently settled." The Illinois senator believed that General George B. McClellan, the new general in chief, had the ability and the means to "soon give us peace."⁴⁸ In addition to being disappointed in Lincoln, Trumbull and many fellow Republicans, with considerable reason, soon found that McClellan was slow and incapable of defeating the rebel armies.

Although morally opposed to slavery, Lincoln, for political and constitutional reasons, did not think that he could include federal emancipation in the Union purpose of the war. He concluded, however, that he must do something to forestall the growing demand for congressional action against slavery that would also satisfy his own antislavery sentiments. In November 1861, he told Browning that he was developing a plan he hoped would satisfy antislavery Republicans and be acceptable to finicky conservatives (moderates in today's lexicon) and border slave Unionists like Crittenden. The plan involved a federally financed and border state approved program of gradual, compensated emancipation that would meet the test of constitutionality and, he believed, soon end the war. Not until March did he put the finishing touches on his plan and submit it to Congress for approval.

Meanwhile, when they met in December, the Republicans had other plans for legislation, which they thought would not challenge the president's prerogatives or disrupt the partnership between the two branches of the government, but would assert congressional authority in formulating federal policy.

CONGRESSIONAL ACTIVISM

On December 2, 1861, the Thirty-Seventh Congress convened for its second session. The Senate consisted of 31 Republicans, 6 Northern or Pacific Coast Democrats, and 11 slave state Unionists (5 old-line Whigs and 5 Democrats, plus a temporarily vacant seat). Although subject to error, an 1862 almanac identified 106 Republicans, 42 Democrats, and 28 Unionists in the House of Representatives.[1]

The next day, Lincoln sent his annual message to Congress, where a clerk read it to the members. He mainly based his message on the annual reports of his department heads, though he drew his own conclusions and made modest recommendations. The president began his message with a somewhat perplexing account of foreign affairs and commerce, which, he reported, "has been attended with profound solicitude." Although Lincoln did not mention the specific reason for his "solicitude," he probably had in mind the crisis with Great Britain caused by the USS *San Jacinto*'s stoppage on November 8 of the British merchant ship *Trent* on the high seas and the forced removal of two Confederate emissaries. The *Trent* Affair, as it was called, between the two countries was resolved in late December.[2]

Lincoln next turned to domestic affairs in his annual message. He indicated that the Treasury had been "conducted with signal success" since Congress's adjournment in August. As he did for other executive departments, the president referred Congress to the secretary of the Treasury's report for a detailed account of that department's activities. In his summary, however, Lincoln showed his affinity for numbers in describing the good condition of the U.S. Treasury.[3]

The president made several suggestions for Congress's consideration. He recommended "that an agricultural and statistical bureau might profitably be organized." He explained, "Agriculture, confessedly the largest interest of the nation has, not a department, nor a bureau, but a clerkship only, assigned to it in the government." Lincoln said that it was "fortunate that this great interest is so independent in its nature as to not have demanded and extorted more from the government." Still, he "respectfully asked Congress to consider whether something more cannot be given voluntarily" to farmers "with general advantage." He specifically thought that "annual reports exhibiting the condition of our agriculture, commerce, and [also] manufactures would present a fund of great practical value to the country."[4]

Not until May did Congress consider Lincoln's recommendation for an agricultural and statistical bureau. A bill was introduced to create a full-blown Department of Agriculture, instead of the smaller bureau that the president had suggested. In the Senate, influential opposition arose against the bill. Both Fessenden and Collamer argued that the department, if established, would grow and become exorbitant in its demands on the U.S. Treasury. They also reminded their colleagues that the president had not asked for a separate department. Abuse would be inevitable, Fessenden predicted; furthermore, he said, farmers did not want it.[5]

The bill creating the Department of Agriculture, however, was approved by both houses of Congress, and Lincoln signed it. In the Senate, strange bedfellows could be found among the 25 senators who voted in favor of the bill and 13 in opposition. Conservative border state senators unanimously voted for the department, along with such radicals as Sumner, Wade, and Wilson of Massachusetts. On the other hand, Fessenden, Collamer, and several of their more conservative Republican colleagues and Northern Democrats opposed the bill.[6]

Lincoln, in his annual message of December 1861, expressed concern regarding the increasing problem of what to do with slaves seized from rebel owners under the Confiscation Act of August. He indicated that those black people who had been liberated, as well as others, had become "dependent upon the United States, and must be provided for in some way." Furthermore, he feared that "some of the States" will pass laws "for their own benefit respectively, and by operation of which persons of the same class [namely, black refugees] will be thrown upon them for disposal." The president recommended that Congress provide for the acceptance of such persons from the states "according to some mode of valuation, in lieu, *pro tanto*, of direct taxes, or upon some other plan to be agreed on with such States." They should, he said, on "acceptance by the general government, be at once deemed free; and . . . in any event, steps [should] be taken for colonizing both classes . . . at some place, or places, in a climate congenial to them. It might be well to consider, too,—whether the free colored people already in the United States could not, so far as individuals may desire, be included in such colonization."[7]

The president admitted to Congress that "to carry out the plan of colonization may involve the acquiring of territory, and also the appropriation of money beyond that to be expended in the territorial acquisition." In justifying the proposal, he tied colonization to the war effort. Lincoln asked, "On this whole proposition,—including the appropriation of money with the acquisition of territory, does not the expediency amount to absolute necessity—that, without which the government itself cannot be perpetuated?"[8] He did not explain why?

Lincoln then wrote, "The war continues. . . . I have been anxious and careful that the inevitable conflict for this purpose shall not degenerate into a violent and remorseless revolutionary struggle. I have, therefore, in every case, thought it proper to keep the integrity of the Union prominent as the primary object of the contest on our part, leaving all questions which are not of vital military importance to the more deliberate action of the legislature." Lincoln informed Congress that in implementing the Confiscation Act of August, he had obeyed "the dictates of prudence," though if Congress saw fit to pass "a new law upon the same subject . . . its propriety will be duly considered." He emphasized that "the Union must be preserved, and hence, all indispensable means must be employed." Nonetheless, the president warned, "We should not be in haste to determine that radical and extreme measures, which may reach the loyal as well as the disloyal, are indispensable."[9]

Republicans in Congress soon moved to pressure the president to take vigorous measures to seize and free slaves and confiscate other forms of rebel property. In addition, they sought to end slavery in the District of Columbia. On the opening day of the session, December 2, 1861, James Eliot of Massachusetts rose on the floor of the House of Representatives and offered a resolution beseeching, not demanding, that the president as commander in chief, in order to save the Union, direct his officers "to emancipate all persons held as slaves in any military district in a state of insurrection."[10] Likewise, Thaddeus Stevens and Owen Lovejoy, Lincoln's Illinois abolitionist friend, offered their own resolutions urging the president to take steps against slavery, including issuing orders for his officers to cease the return of fugitive slaves to their masters. The resolutions were held over for future debate.[11] As historian Allen C. Guelzo has noted, "[The] repeated clamors for action in Congress" at this time were "very narrow [in] scope. No one seriously proposed laying hands on slavery in the Border states, much less abolishing the institution of slavery."[12] Nonetheless, radicals Charles Sumner in the Senate and James M. Ashley of Ohio in the House soon set to work drafting resolutions that would require abolition as a part of any reconstruction plan for the seceded states.[13]

Two days after the antislavery resolutions were introduced by Stevens and Lovejoy, and then held over for possible consideration, Lyman Trumbull stirred up a hornet's nest in the Senate when he introduced a confiscation bill that was far more stringent than the one of 1861. Trumbull's bill provided for "the absolute and complete forfeiture . . . of every species of property, real and personal . . . belonging to persons [who] shall take up arms against the United States, or in any wise aid or abet the rebellion." Slaves confiscated by the army, according to the proposed bill, would immediately be freed without the owner's benefit of due process of law. Owners who claimed to be Unionists would have to prove their loyalty before recovering their slaves. The bill was ordered to be printed and referred to the Judiciary Committee, which Trumbull chaired.[14]

When the confiscation bill came up for debate in March 1862, a broad range of senators opposed it. In addition to border state conservatives and Northern Democrats, several Republican senators objected to the bill on constitutional grounds and also because, they argued, its passage would increase support for the rebels in the slave states. In a long speech in the Senate on March 4, Senator Edgar Cowan of Pennsylvania declared that the proposed law violated the due process clause in the Constitution and was a bill of attainder, which was unconstitutional. "Pass this bill," he thundered, "and all that is left of the Constitution is not worth much." Cowan reminded the Senate that the war was "waged solely for the Constitution, and for the ends, aims, and purposes sanctioned by it, and for no others." Furthermore, if the bill were enacted, "the same messenger who carries it to the South will come back to us with the news of their complete consolidation as a man" behind the rebellion.[15]

With less fervor and exaggeration, Senator Collamer of Vermont made a similar argument against Trumbull's confiscation bill.[16] Cowan, Collamer, and other Republican opponents of the bill were well aware of Lincoln's admonition in his annual message not to be in haste to adopt "radical and extreme measures." The president had confiscation legislation in mind as an example of a radical measure that should be avoided. Still, true to his "political education" as a former Whig, he did not intrude in the congressional debate over Trumbull's proposal until a revised bill was ready for his action in July.

Meanwhile, in March 1862, Lincoln drafted a gradual, compensated emancipation scheme for the border slave states, a proposal that he had pondered since November. He believed that his plan would meet the test of constitutionality, retain executive control of the slavery issue, and bring about an early end to the war. On March 6, the president submitted his proposal to Congress for its consideration in the form of a resolution, which read, "Resolve that the United States ought to co-operate with any state which may adopt gradual abolishment of slavery, giving to such state pecuniary aid, to be used by such state in it's [sic] discretion, to compensate for the inconveniences public and private, produced by such change of system." He promised, however, "If the proposition . . . does not meet the approval of Congress and the country, there is the end" of it. Lincoln referred the members of Congress to the U.S. census tables and Treasury reports before them and argued that they should readily see "how very soon the current expenditures of the war would purchase, at fair valuation, all the slaves in any named State." The approval of the plan, he said, would deprive the rebels of the border states support for the war, and they would realize that their cause was hopeless. Thus it "substantially ends the rebellion," he optimistically predicted.[17]

In order to make the plan palatable for the border states, which had to approve it, the president announced that these Union states need not abolish slavery immediately. They could adopt a plan for the "initiation" of abolition "because," he said, "in my judgment, gradual, and not sudden emancipation, is better for all." Lincoln insisted that the proposal "sets up no claim of a right, by federal authority, to interfere with slavery within state limits, referring, as it does, the absolute control of the subject, in each case, to the state and it's [*sic*] people. . . . It is proposed as a matter of perfectly free choice."[18]

The president's compensated emancipation scheme received broad support in the North, undercutting the efforts of Senator Sumner and Representative Ashley to make abolition a requirement for Southern reconstruction. Lincoln's proposal also had the effect of complicating Senator Trumbull's attempts to secure early passage of his confiscation bill. The *New York Times*, a Republican newspaper, published several articles and editorials praising Lincoln's resolutions. It asserted that the president "has hit the happy mean upon which all parties in the North and all loyalists in the South can unite." Horace Greeley's *New York Tribune* approved the plan and proclaimed it the first step toward emancipation. The Washington correspondent of the *New York World*, a Democratic newspaper, reported from the capital that the president's proposal was "generally regarded as a most ingenious and timely political movement," which, he wrote, had silenced the radical clamor in Congress for immediate emancipation.[19]

It soon became clear, however, that the key players in Lincoln's compensated emancipation plan—those from the border states both in Congress and in the state legislatures—refused to participate in it.

Having received reports of the opposition of border state members of Congress to the proposal, Lincoln called them to the White House for the purpose of persuading them to support the plan. The meeting occurred on March 10, and it quickly became a freewheeling discussion of the president's resolution, led by John J. Crittenden. The Kentucky congressman told Lincoln that border state members of Congress feared that approval of the proposal would be an entering wedge for direct federal intervention against slavery in the South, which, they insisted, would be unconstitutional and would prolong the war. Lincoln tried unsuccessfully to reassure them that this would not be the case. He reiterated that if the border states accepted the plan, rebel hopes for success "would be removed, and more would be accomplished towards shortening the war than could be hoped from the greatest victory achieved by Union armies." When Representative William A. Hall of Missouri asked the president about his personal opinion of slavery, Lincoln answered that "he thought it was wrong and [would] continue to think so; but that was not the question" to be dealt with at this time.[20]

Although probably few members of Congress believed Lincoln's assertion that approval of the plan would substantially shorten the war, Republicans saw it as a hopeful and constitutional way, without violating states' rights, to begin ending slavery in the South. Two days after the president met with the border state congressmen, the House of Representatives passed the compensated emancipation resolution by a vote of 97 to 36, with the border state members and Northern Democrats voting overwhelmingly against it.[21]

The action of the Senate on Lincoln's resolution was delayed by the consideration of a bill, introduced by Senator Henry Wilson in December, to abolish slavery in the District of Columbia. The bill was immediately calendared for debate in March. On March 24, Lincoln expressed concern in a letter to Horace Greeley that the debate over slavery in the District would complicate the acceptance of his border state plan. The president told the *New York Tribune* editor that he would be more favorable to "the abolishment of slavery in this District . . . if some one or more of the border-states would move fast toward approving the compensation offer."[22] Even before

Congress had completed its action on the District emancipation bill, and despite efforts of border state senators to secure a black colonization requirement in Lincoln's plan, the Senate on April 2 passed the president's compensated emancipation resolution by a vote of 32 to 10. Congress, however, had agreed only in principle to the scheme; it awaited the decision of the border states before considering approval of the bonds for actual reimbursement to the slaveholders. The sticking point for any further action therefore rested with the border state legislatures, which seemed hostile from the beginning to the plan.

Meanwhile, debate in Congress focused on the historic bill to abolish slavery in the District of Columbia, where many members believed that the federal government had constitutional authority to act against the institution. On March 12, Lot Morrill of Maine, a member of the Committee on District Affairs, brought the bill to the Senate floor. A brief but lively debate immediately broke out, with the border state senators vehemently opposing the measure. Lazarus W. Powell of Kentucky denounced the bill, despite a compensation provision, as unconstitutional in that it would deprive the slave owners of their property without due process of law. Garret Davis of Kentucky, a staunch Unionist and former Whig congressman who had replaced John C. Breckinridge in the Senate, made the most impassioned—and extreme—case against the District abolition bill. Davis, who owned fifteen slaves in 1860, declared that the bill's passage would lead to a racial conflagration in the South. He predicted a "bloody Vendee in the whole of the slave States," as had occurred in the French Revolution, if Congress and the president approved the measure.[23] When the debate resumed on March 24–25, Republican James Harlan of Iowa countered Davis's dire prediction by insisting, "There is no danger of this war of extermination," as Davis feared, or that the former slaves would murder their former masters. They would continue to labor as before, Harlan said.[24]

Knowing that several Republican senators, including James Doolittle of Wisconsin, favored the colonization of freed black people, Davis offered an amendment to the District bill that required resettlement of the emancipated slaves outside of the United States.[25] Doolittle and other conservative Republicans had been influenced, at least partly, by the president's endorsement of the principle of colonization in his annual message to Congress. However, like Lincoln, these Republican senators opposed the forced resettlement of black people. In favoring some form of black colonization, whether voluntary or compulsory, senators on both sides of the aisle, especially those from the West (today's Midwest), had received reports from their constituents of the bitter opposition to the prospect of freed black people flooding their communities and creating racial conflict.

The Davis amendment almost passed in the Senate when it came to a vote on March 24. The balloting ended in a tie, broken by Vice President Hannibal Hamlin's vote against it. Senator Doolittle offered a counterproposal that would provide $100,000 to aid the voluntary colonization of freed slaves, a position that Lincoln favored. The Doolittle amendment passed. Davis, however, continued to rail against the District emancipation bill, if it did not contain a compulsory removal provision.[26]

The tide clearly turned in favor of the District emancipation bill in the Senate when William Pitt Fessenden on April 1 made a persuasive appeal for its passage. He especially attempted to allay conservative and Democratic fears that the abolition of slavery in the District of Columbia would lead to congressional emancipation in the slave states. Fessenden admitted that "the Republican party would rejoice to see slavery abolished everywhere," and he himself desired that it should occur "as soon as may be, by constitutional methods." He fancifully hoped that "a party [might] arise and become a majority" in the slave states that would act against slavery. The Maine senator, however, reassured concerned conservatives "that the Congress of the United States . . . under the Constitution, as it exists now, have no right whatever to touch, by legislation, the institution of slavery in the States where it exists by law." Nonetheless, he said, Congress had the constitutional power to weaken slavery by subjecting it to the laws of the land and by taking away its political influence in the country. Ending slavery in the District would be an important step in that direction, Fessenden announced.[27]

Two days later, the bill to abolish slavery in the national capital passed the Senate by a vote of 29 to 14. Voting against it were the border state senators, now including Willey and Carlile of the Restored Government of Virginia, and also five western Democrats. Senator James Pearce of Maryland was sick and absent, and Senator Edgar Cowan of Pennsylvania, who might have voted against the bill, was also absent.[28] The debate on the District emancipation bill now shifted to the House of Representatives, where, after the Senate's overwhelming approval of it, border state and Democratic opponents faced a virtually hopeless task.

In the House on April 11, Crittenden made a passionate speech against the bill in a desperate effort to prevent its passage. He reminded his colleagues that the masses of Southern people supported the rebellion because of apprehension that Congress under Republican leadership would act to free the slaves in the South. The introduction in Congress of the District of Columbia emancipation bill, Crittenden declared, had reinforced this fear. Its enactment, he insisted, would cause the rebels (which also included his grandson) to "fight with greater fury" to achieve their independence. His appeal, however, probably changed few votes. On the same day, the House approved the bill by a vote of 92 to 39.[29] For the first time in American history, Congress had taken a direct step against slavery.[30]

On April 14, Senator Browning took the District emancipation bill to the White House for his friend's action. Lincoln informed him that he would sign it, although, as he told Browning, he "regretted the bill had been passed" without providing for gradual emancipation. In approving the bill on April 16, the president sent a revealing message to Congress. He indicated, "I have never doubted the constitutional authority of congress to abolish slavery in this District; and I have ever desired to see the national capital freed from the institution in some satisfactory way. Hence there has never been, in my mind, any question upon the subject, except the one of expediency, arising in view of all the circumstances." Lincoln did not specify the "circumstances" he had in mind. However, he probably meant the failure of the District bill to provide for gradual freedom and its poor timing in view of the border states' consideration of his compensated emancipation proposal. Nonetheless, he was "gratified that the two principles of compensation, and colonization, [were] both recognized, and practically applied in the act." The president also expressed his regret that the bill had omitted any provision for "minors, femes-covert, insane, or absent persons," and he requested supplementary legislation to correct the problem. Congress later approved his suggestion.[31]

By the spring of 1862, Senator Trumbull's confiscation bill, after endless debate and amendments, seemed destined to fail. Conservative Republicans joined Democrats and border state Unionists in opposing any provision that could be construed to annul an owner's property rights without recourse to judicial proceedings. At the same time, border slave state legislatures had demonstrated no intention of adopting the president's gradual compensated emancipation plan. Faced with increased financial demands to support the war, Congress had failed to appropriate the money that Lincoln hoped would spur the border state legislatures to approve his proposal.

Meanwhile, attention in Washington became focused on the critical military operations in Virginia and elsewhere. With high hopes, General George B. McClellan had launched a campaign in the spring to take Richmond and end the war. By July, his massive army, which Republicans now derisively referred to as "McClellan's body guard," had bogged down in the Peninsula Campaign near the Confederate capital and soon faced a humiliating retreat. Demoralization pervaded the army and the North. Reports of the large numbers of casualties and desertions in the army inevitably created problems for the War Department's recruitment efforts to replace the losses. Lincoln's call for three hundred thousand additional volunteers on July 1 met with little enthusiasm, though the Union governors sanguinely promised that they would raise the quotas for their states.[32]

On July 8, Henry Wilson, chairman of the Senate Committee on Military Affairs, introduced a bill to authorize the president to call out the state militias for a total of three hundred thousand men for nine months. If the states failed to meet their quotas, militia drafting would occur. But this could be avoided by the states filling their ranks with volunteers. A potentially radical feature of Wilson's militia bill was the provision authorizing the president "to receive into the service of the United States, for the purpose of constructing intrenchments [*sic*], or performing camp service, or any other labor, or any military or naval service for which they may be found competent, persons of African descent."[33] If the Massachusetts senator had consulted beforehand with Lincoln on the bill, or talked to Senator Browning, he would have known that the president opposed the use of black men as soldiers, though he probably had no reservations about their employment as laborers in the army. On July 1, Lincoln had read a paper to Browning in which he declared that the arming of African Americans "would produce dangerous & fatal dissatisfaction in our army, and do more injury than good."[34]

Senator Wilson had hardly introduced his militia bill when slave-state senators Willard Saulsbury and John S. Carlile were on their feet to denounce it. The provision to put black men in the military, Saulsbury claimed, not only was unconstitutional but also had broken the promise of the president and Congress that the war would be fought only to preserve the Union as it had been. Carlile, a senator of the rump Union government of Virginia, echoed this view and added that "the effect of such legislation will be to degrade the white man to the level of the negro." Just as quickly, John Sherman of Ohio, William Pitt Fessenden, and other Republican senators came to the defense of Wilson's bill because of the tremendous need for manpower in the army. They argued that the bill was actually an amendment to the Uniform Militia Act of 1792, was constitutional, and would not lead to black rights as its opponents claimed. The question now, Sherman told the Senate, was "whether the people of the United States, struggling for national existence, should employ these blacks for the maintenance of the Government."[35]

On July 15, the Senate gave its answer: it passed the militia bill. The next day, the House approved it.[36] The bill passed both houses by a comfortable majority, with some Northern Democrats voting for it. Because the bill did not require the president to enlist black men in the military and its implementation remained in the hands of state authorities, Lincoln had few qualms about signing it. Nonetheless, the Militia Act of 1862 became the first step toward the nationalization of the army and also toward military conscription.[37] In addition, the act recognized the official role of black people in the Union struggle, leading to their service in the militia of supportive states like Massachusetts. In his Emancipation Proclamation on January 1, 1863, Lincoln dropped his disapproval of black troops and authorized their recruitment.

The decision on Senator Lyman Trumbull's confiscation bill, which was more stringent than the one of August 1861, finally occurred in July 1862, but only after bitter debate. Congress was sharply divided over the bill, with several Republican senators joining Northern Democrats and border state Unionists in opposition. Opponents denounced the bill's sweeping confiscation features, which included virtually all rebel property, and insisted that its passage would increase support for the rebellion in the South. They also repeated their claim that it was unconstitutional because it denied due process of law for aggrieved owners. During early 1862, the debate on the bill and its amendments continued intermittently. Finally, on May 26, the House of Representatives, pressed by radicals like Thaddeus Stevens and Owen Lovejoy, passed a modified version of the bill by a vote of 82 to 68, with nine Republicans along with most Democrats and border state Unionists opposing it.[38]

The Senate, however, refused to approve the House version, whereupon the two chambers formed a conference committee to resolve the differences. The bill that came out of the committee was essentially the same as the House measure. It was vigorously supported in the Senate by radicals such as Sumner and Wade. Nonetheless, Republican senator Daniel Clark of New Hampshire offered a substitute that had earlier been considered by the Senate and was less radical than the House bill. A raucous debate erupted over the two versions of the bill, with Clark and conservative Republicans Browning and Cowan announcing that they could never vote for the House proposal.[39]

In the course of the debate, Republican senator Morton S. Wilkinson of Minnesota leveled his rhetorical guns on Browning. He castigated the Illinois senator—and friend of Lincoln—for his "hostility to a measure which is calculated to make the guilty authors of all this suffering and of all this crime bear some portion of the burdens which he is so ready to place upon the shoulders of the liberty-loving citizens of the loyal States of the Union." Wilkinson asked, "Why is it that [Browning] is so sensitive when the interests of traitors are attacked, and yet so ready to [sacrifice] the property and the blood of Union men like water to save the Union?" As expected, Browning denounced his fellow Republican for his intemperate remarks and boasted, "The country will rejoice to know that there was more of sympathy between the Administration of the country and myself than there was between the Senator of Minnesota and the Administration."[40]

Three days later, Browning talked with Lincoln, after which he wrote in his diary, "He read me a paper embodying his views of the objects of the war, and the proper mode for conducting it in its relations to slavery. This, he told me, he had sketched hastily with the intention of laying it before the Cabinet. His views coincided entirely with my own." These presumably related to the issue of confiscation of rebel property, including slaves.[41]

In the end, the debate in the Senate had a moderating effect in both houses. Most conservative Republicans now supported a compromise measure, but diehard radicals such as Sumner and Wade did not. Section 6 in the new bill made it palatable for the majority of senators; it provided that before the seizure of the property of rebels, the president should give a sixty-day warning for them to cease their aid of the rebellion. The bill also included a provision authorizing the president to foster voluntary black colonization, preferably in a foreign land. On July 11, the confiscation bill passed the House of Representatives by a vote of 82 to 42; the next day, the Senate gave its approval, 28 to 13.[42]

A sticking point for the enactment of the confiscation bill of 1862 was President Lincoln. Earlier the president had refused to interfere in the debate on the issue, but by the summer he had become increasingly concerned about some of the bill's provisions. He particularly found troubling the fact that the bill did not explicitly prohibit the confiscation of property beyond the lifetime of the offender. Lincoln also found disturbing the bill's failure to permit judicial hearings for alleged rebels whose property had been confiscated. In addition, he thought that the bill's timing, as in the case of the District of Columbia antislavery bill in the spring, would undercut his efforts to secure the border states' acceptance of his compensated emancipation proposal.

On July 14, Browning again met with the president and vigorously expressed his opposition to the confiscation bill. He urged Lincoln to veto the measure when it arrived on his desk, arguing that the bill was unconstitutional and certain to lose border state and Northern Democratic support if it became law. Furthermore, Browning told Lincoln that the president "had reached the culminating point in his administration, and his course upon the bill was to determine whether he was to control the abolitionists and radicals, or whether they were to control him." The president promised his Illinois friend that "he would give [the bill] his profound consideration."[43] Browning had exaggerated the political effect that a failure by Lincoln to veto the bill would have, since public sentiment in the North had come to favor a law that forced the rebels to pay for continuing the war.

A report had reached Congress that the president was preparing a veto message on the confiscation bill. This disturbing news sent Senator Fessenden and other Republican supporters of the measure scurrying to the White House to talk to Lincoln. Although they had a comfortable majority for approving the bill, Republican leaders knew that a presidential veto would doom it. Several members in the Senate and a larger number in the House who had reluctantly voted for the bill would likely follow the president's lead and sustain the veto. Both Lincoln and the Republicans in Congress understood that the failure to enact it would contribute to more divisions in the party and with the public when Union forces were incurring serious setbacks in the South.

Congress and the president quickly worked out a solution to their differences over the bill that Congress had approved on July 11. After talking to Lincoln, and while he was completing the draft of a veto message, Republican congressional leaders on July 15 hurriedly secured the passage of a joint explanatory resolution that was designed to satisfy the president's main objections to the bill. Nonetheless, two days later, Lincoln submitted to Congress the draft of his veto message that contained his objections—and also his support—of provisions in the bill that he wanted Congress to consider. Significantly, he did not threaten to veto the bill.

Lincoln informed Congress that an important objection to the bill was that it failed to make provision "for determining whether a particular individual slave does or does not fall within the [offending] classes" of slaveholders. The president complained that the bill also failed to provide an owner whose property had been seized a reasonable period of time for a court hearing on the question of his loyalty. This neglect, the president said, would prevent a loyal owner from reclaiming his property. Even more important, Lincoln objected to the fact that the bill lacked a provision explicitly stating that the forfeiture of the property would not extend beyond the lifetime of the offender. In neither case did Congress act on Lincoln's concern. Although opposed to black troops in the military, the president approved the clause authorizing him, through his military commanders, "to employ as laborers, as many persons of African de[s]cent, as can be used to advantage."[44] He implicitly endorsed the provision for voluntary black colonization, a policy established earlier in the District of Columbia emancipation bill.

With the president's approval on July 17, the Second Confiscation Act, as it is known, became law. Historian John Syrett concluded that the confiscation legislation "accomplished little," writing, "It was a poorly designed measure without an enforcement mechanism," which neither the Lincoln administration nor Congress had much interest in implementing.[45] Lincoln had a more realistic and immediate use for the Second Confiscation Act—to justify his issuance of the Emancipation Proclamation he had been contemplating.

On July 22, Lincoln brought to a cabinet meeting the first draft of his Emancipation Proclamation. He began the document by citing as his authority the sixth section of the Second Confiscation Act, which directed the president to issue a proclamation giving a sixty-day warning for rebels to cease their insurrection or their property would be liable to seizure. He also cited his military responsibility as commander in chief for the prosecution of the war. In his draft proclamation, Lincoln indicated that on January 1, 1863, he would issue an order freeing "slaves within any state or states" still in rebellion. In a subsequent cabinet meeting on July 25, the president agreed with Secretary of State Seward that he should withhold the proclamation until a Union victory had been achieved on the battlefield.[46] On September 22, after the Battle of Antietam, Lincoln issued a preliminary Emancipation Proclamation announcing his purpose to free the slaves on January 1 in rebel states or in Southern congressional districts that had shown no intention of returning to the Union. However, it was the Republican Congress, as had been the case with the District of Columbia emancipation bill, that had taken the initiative toward ending slavery; the president, willing but slow, had followed its lead.

The second session of the Thirty-Seventh Congress also took action on three important nonmilitary issues. It did so with little input from President Lincoln in either the proceedings or debates on the proposals. However, the appropriate congressional committees often consulted with members of his administration on the legislation. Although these measures were not directly related to the prosecution of the war, they had lasting significance, and all had their origins before the conflict. The Republican platform of 1860 had strongly endorsed two of these measures: free homesteads for settlers and a railroad from the Mississippi Valley to the Pacific.

The free homestead movement dated back to the 1840s. Support for it picked up momentum during the 1850s, only to be resisted by Democrats in Congress, including Southerners who linked it with the antislavery free soil crusade. Opponents were joined by northeastern congressmen who could see no benefit for their states to homestead legislation. Nonetheless, with growing Republican support, a homestead bill passed Congress in 1859, but it was vetoed by President James Buchanan, a Democrat. On February 12, 1861, at Cincinnati, President-elect Lincoln announced to a crowd mainly of German immigrants that a homestead law was "worthy of consideration, and that the wild lands of the country should be distributed so that every man should have the means and opportunity of benefitting his condition." However, he made no specific recommendation.[47]

In December 1861, after Southern opponents withdrew from Congress, Republican Owen Lovejoy of Illinois introduced in the House of Representatives the same homestead bill that Buchanan had vetoed. In the debate on the legislation, a nonpartisan alignment developed, which often happened when regional interests were involved, in this case western interests. Clement Vallandigham, the emerging Ohio Copperhead leader, joined the staunchly antislavery Lovejoy and other Republicans in support of the homestead measure.[48] The bill provided 160 acres of free land for each settler upon payment of a modest fee. Title to the land would be granted only after five years of the homesteader's living on the property and making improvements.

Congressional consideration of the measure soon became entangled in the issue of outright land bounties for Union soldiers. The problem was resolved by a provision that those men who had served at least two years could receive title to the land after one year. This concession influenced many northeastern congressmen, with land-hungry soldiers to satisfy, to support the legislation. On May 7, 1862, the House approved the homestead bill by a vote of 82 to 41; the Senate followed suit by a margin of 27 to 12. As expected, President Lincoln signed the bill. The Homestead Act, however, did not prove to be the boon for the landless that had been anticipated by its sponsors; by 1900, less than 4 percent of the lands west of the Mississippi River had been taken up by homesteaders.[49] Railroads, land companies, and corporations received the lion's share of the available land.

The effort to secure a railroad connecting the Mississippi Valley with the Pacific, to include federal aid for its construction, also reached fruition in mid-1862. Before the war, the proposal for a transcontinental railroad had been stymied in Congress by constitutional concerns, especially by Democrats whose states would be little affected by the road. Furthermore, divisions regarding funding and land grants for construction of the railway also created divisions. Disputes over the terminus of the line in the Mississippi Valley further complicated congressional action on the proposed railroad. But like the movement for free homestead legislation, momentum for a Pacific railroad grew. In 1860, the Republican platform and the Democratic platforms of both Stephen A. Douglas and John C. Breckinridge supported it. Although not all Southerners opposed the railroad, the withdrawal of their delegations in 1861 increased the likelihood that Congress would approve the project.

Furthermore, congressional supporters of the Pacific railway could be virtually ensured that when Lincoln became president, he would sign the legislation designed to aid the project. The rapid development of his state's interior during the 1850s had given Lincoln a firsthand opportunity to witness the benefits of federal land grants in the construction of the Illinois Central Railroad. Although his rival, Senator Douglas, had been the leading supporter of the Illinois Central, Lincoln as a Henry Clay Whig was friendlier to public aid for internal improvements than were the Democrats. He also had served as an attorney in railroad cases, both for and against the companies; he understood their importance and the problems associated with their development. Furthermore, Lincoln took seriously the promise in the Republican platform to provide federal support for the Pacific railroad project.

When the Thirty-Seventh Congress met for its first session in July 1861, western congressmen moved to fulfill the dream of a transcontinental railroad. In the House, where funding had to begin for it, Republican Samuel R. Curtis of Iowa, soon to be a Union general, secured the appointment of a select committee to study and propose a Pacific railway bill for consideration by the members. In the Senate, Democrat James A. McDougall of California also received approval for a similar committee. Along with other western champions of the railroad, McDougall insisted that its construction was necessary for the prosecution of the war.[50] Although they probably exaggerated the importance of the road's completion in the suppression of the rebellion, westerners argued that the rebel closure of the lower Mississippi River to western commerce made urgent its construction. More immediate matters relating to the war, however, occupied Congress's attention during its brief 1861 summer session. Furthermore, the select committees needed considerable time to study and work out the details, which included resolving the competing interests in the project. Also, the president, true to his Whig education regarding the separation of powers, and despite his support for the Pacific railroad, did not use his influence to push for congressional action on the proposal.

After several postponements of the issue, the House of Representatives on April 8, 1862, began consideration of a Pacific railway bill offered by Republican James H. Campbell of Pennsylvania, chairman of the House select committee to study its feasibility. Conflict occurred over several issues—the terminus of the railroad, proposals for the railroad's branches, the extent of federal funds and land for its construction, and the timing for such an ambitious project while the war was in progress. As chairman of the powerful House Committee on Ways and Means, Thaddeus Stevens insisted that his committee should have an important role in determining the extent of federal aid for the railroad. Furthermore, he warned on May 6, "If the disagreement among the western and northwestern members should [continue to] clog the bill," particularly over "further branches and other lines, it cannot have my support." He reminded House members "that this is not a western measure, and ought not to be defended as such." The construction of the transcontinental railroad, Stevens declared, vitally concerned the commerce and industries of the East, as well as western development.[51]

Sobered by Stevens's admonition, the House on the same day passed the Pacific railway bill by a vote of 79 to 49.[52] No clear partisan or sectional division can be detected in support of the measure. Despite wrangling over its details and amendments (such as the railroad's eastern terminus), the Senate passed the bill on June 20 by an overwhelming margin of 35 to 5. Four days later, the House accepted amendments by the Senate, and the president signed the Pacific Railway Act on July 1.[53]

The act provided for the construction of a railroad from Omaha to the San Francisco Bay area. It granted sixty-four hundred acres of public land (later doubled) and $16,000 in federal loans for every mile of track completed. Moving in different directions, the Union Pacific and the Central Pacific Railroad Companies eventually linked their tracks at Promontory, Utah, in 1869, thereby completing the first transcontinental line. Already in 1864, Congress passed and President Lincoln signed a bill creating the Northern Pacific Railroad and approved even larger land grants for the construction of a road from St. Paul to Seattle.[54]

The third important nonmilitary measure passed by Congress and signed by the president in 1862 was the Land-Grant College Act. Except perhaps for the GI Bill of Rights at the end of the Second World War, no law has had a greater impact on higher education in America than this act. Like the free homestead and Pacific railroad movements, the effort to obtain federal backing for the establishment of agricultural and mechanical institutions of education began before the Civil War, during the 1840s. In 1859, Republican congressman Justin Smith Morrill of Vermont secured the passage of a land grant college bill, only to have it vetoed by President Buchanan. Although the Republican platform of 1860 had not included support for the bill, Morrill continued to demand its passage.

When the Thirty-Seventh Congress convened in its second session in December 1861, Morrill reintroduced his land-grant college bill in the House. The bill provided thirty thousand acres of land for each state's U.S. Senate and House member to establish a college for the study of agriculture, mechanical arts, and "military tactics." The inclusion of military science, which Morrill justified as a war measure, would make the grant of federal land constitutionally acceptable to concerned members of Congress and also the public. The land would be sold by the states in land scrip and invested in "safe stock" for the intended purposes of the law. Morrill's bill was referred to the Committee on Public Works, where it languished for five months, mainly because of a lack of western enthusiasm for it. Some western members believed that the eastern states where colleges already existed would reap the benefits of the bill and also profit from its financing.[55]

Before the House acted on the land-grant college bill, Morrill persuaded Ben Wade to introduce the bill in the Senate, which he did on May 19. After Senator James Harlan of Iowa reassured Senator

James H. Lane of Kansas that the bill would not prevent the enactment of the Pacific railway measure, which both supported, the Senate on June 10 approved the land-grant college bill, 32 to 7. One week later, the House passed it by a vote of 90 to 25.[56]

One day after signing the Pacific Railway Act, Lincoln on July 2 approved the Land-Grant College Act. Two weeks later, the second session of the Thirty-Seventh Congress adjourned, having achieved a remarkable legislative record, largely with the cooperation of the Lincoln administration and despite a serious disagreement with the president over the Second Confiscation Act. The differences were resolved through a compromise and the desire, even by non-Republicans in Congress, to cooperate as much as their constituents and political principles would permit in order to avoid unnecessary divisions over legislation that could undermine the government's war effort. Lincoln's relationship with Congress, however, would soon be tested, as the war in late 1862 continued to go badly for the Union, Northern morale plummeted, and the Republican Party suffered important setbacks in the fall elections. The president's preliminary Emancipation Proclamation and his suspension of the writ of habeas corpus in September were politically ill timed and contributed to a growing belief by Republicans in Congress as well as border state Unionists and Northern Democrats that Lincoln was incapable of leading the nation through its greatest crisis.

A TIME OF DESPAIR

By the fall of 1862, Union military fortunes had reached a low point, creating serious public disillusionment with the war and with the president's leadership. After General McClellan's failure in the Peninsula Campaign in midsummer against General Lee, President Lincoln brought General John Pope from the West to command the armies in Virginia. The brash Pope, who was the darling of the Radical Republicans, announced that he would make short work of "Bobby Lee." In the Battle of Second Bull Run in late August, Pope and the Union forces suffered a humiliating defeat. Much to the dismay of Republicans and members of the president's cabinet, Lincoln restored McClellan to the command of the army in the East as Lee's forces began an invasion of Maryland. Although McClellan checked the Confederates at Antietam on September 17, in Lincoln's mind, he had failed to take advantage of his success by destroying Lee's army before it returned to Virginia.

A somewhat similar military situation developed in the western theater (Mississippi Valley), where Confederate forces under Braxton Bragg and Edmund Kirby Smith had penetrated the Bluegrass State, brushed aside Union troops, and reached the banks of the Ohio River before confronting General Don Carlos Buell at Perryville in central Kentucky on October 8. Although Buell succeeded in repulsing the Confederate army at Perryville and caused it to retreat to Tennessee, the Union commander, like McClellan in the East, did not follow up on his success. In Missouri and elsewhere, the Union cause staggered in the face of a Confederate resurgence. The seizure of New Orleans by federal naval and military forces in May had been virtually the only bright spot in the war for the Union. By the fall, volunteers for the army had largely dried up, and the Militia Act of July had not achieved the goals that the president and Congress expected. In western states such as Illinois and Indiana, peace supporters urged men not to volunteer or to subject themselves to the militia draft. In some cases, recruiting officers experienced violence at the hands of antiwar activists.

In this foreboding situation, Lincoln issued his preliminary Emancipation Proclamation on September 22, 1862, which he had informed his cabinet that he would do after the Union forces achieved a success on the battlefield. Although he had been disappointed with McClellan's failure to destroy Lee's army in Maryland, Lincoln pronounced the Battle of Antietam a victory and declared that, after a warning, he would free slaves in areas still in rebellion.[1] Such a proclamation, he knew, would be effective only in areas controlled by the Union army as it moved south, and he also knew that it would be controversial.

Lincoln followed his antislavery directive with a sweeping proclamation on September 24 suspending the writ of habeas corpus. Earlier, on August 8, Secretary of War Edwin M. Stanton, after receiving "verbal directions" from the president and fearing that the Militia Act would be resisted, had suspended the writ throughout the country.[2] Lincoln's proclamation provided for the arrest of "all Rebels and Insurgents, their aiders and abettors within the United States, and all persons discouraging voluntary enlistments, resisting militia drafts, or guilty of any disloyal practice." Violators, the president directed, would "be subject to martial law and liable to trial and punishment by Courts Martial or Military Commission."[3]

With important elections scheduled for November and war weariness and dissent soaring, the political situation for the president and the Republicans had become grim. Lincoln's issuance of his emancipation and habeas corpus proclamations made matters worse for his party and for the prosecution of the war, though many Republicans, especially in the upper North, applauded his actions. Democratic leaders such as Horatio Seymour of New York vigorously attacked the two presidential decrees. In the lower North, the proclamations increased support for the Copperheads, the peace faction of the Democratic Party. Conservative Republicans and border state Unionists also expressed concern regarding the legality of the suspension of the writ and the antislavery proclamation. Even Secretary of the Navy Gideon Welles, after reading about the writ's suspension in the newspapers, doubted "the utility of a multiplicity of Proclamations striking deep on great questions" that affected slavery and constitutional liberties.[4]

When Congress reassembled in December 1862, Senator John S. Carlile of Virginia declared that the writ of habeas corpus should never be suspended where the courts were open, a position later taken by the Supreme Court in *Ex parte Milligan* (1866). Senator Trumbull, chairman of the Senate Judiciary Committee, replied that if the writ could not be suspended where courts existed, then practically it could not be suspended at all.[5] On March 3, 1863, Trumbull and his Republican colleagues secured the passage of an ambiguous bill, which Lincoln signed, giving the president the right to suspend the writ. The act, however, provided that political offenders should not be held indefinitely, a safeguard that often was honored in the breech.[6] Lincoln did not take advantage of his new authority until September 15, 1863, when, angered by state courts' attempting to prevent army recruitment and the arrest of deserters, he issued a second proclamation suspending the writ of habeas corpus that was stronger than the 1862 one.

In the fall 1862 elections, Republicans suffered severe losses in New York and elsewhere in the lower North. Seymour won the governorship of the Empire State, and the Indiana and Illinois legislatures fell to his party. Fortunately for Lincoln's party, no gubernatorial elections occurred in Indiana and Illinois, or in Ohio and Pennsylvania, where Democrats captured most of the congressional seats. The Democratic avalanche in Lincoln's home state cost his friend and confidant Orville Browning his seat in the Senate when the new legislature met in early 1863 and replaced him with William A. Richardson. Despite losses, the Republicans, though by a smaller majority than before, held on to both houses of Congress.

In an atmosphere of growing public disillusionment with the war and political uncertainty in the North, the Thirty-Seventh Congress reconvened on December 1, 1862, for its third and final session. Some congressmen feared a political revolution in the lower North if the war continued to go badly and casualties mounted. Indeed, Copperheads in Indiana and Illinois seemed poised to gain control of their legislatures. Unionists in the border slave states had become extremely restive and deeply concerned about what would happen in their states if the president issued the Emancipation Proclamation on January 1. Although Lincoln still dangled his gradual, compensated emancipation plan before the border states, the scheme had virtually no chance of success.

After it assembled, Congress had important old business to take care of first—the question of West Virginia statehood. The Restored Government of Virginia, with Francis H. Pierpont as governor, had been created in 1861 by Unionists in the western part of the state with the intention of granting statehood to the western counties. Meeting in Wheeling, the rump Union legislature of the Old Dominion in May 1862 asked, in the form of a memorial endorsed by Governor Pierpont, for congressional permission to form the state of West Virginia.

On May 29, Virginia senator Waitman T. Willey presented the statehood memorial, or resolution, to the Senate and made a long speech calling for its approval. He announced that the diversity of interests dividing eastern and western Virginia, based on geography and economic development, "[had] been muted for fifty years" and necessitated the formation of the new state. Willey argued that the memorial for West Virginia statehood from the Restored Government reflected the desire of all the Old Dominion's loyal people and not just the Unionists of the western counties. As the body politic of Virginia, the Restored Government, he said, had the constitutional authority to approve the separation of the state. He acknowledged that slavery was not congenial to the area's economy or to "the moral and religious sentiments of the people," but he did not want the issue of statehood "to be entangled in the mazes of arguments with which moralists and religionists have surrounded and involved the question." The new state, Willey insisted, must have "the perfect freedom [to] regulate its own institutions and policy, in conformity with local exigencies and interests peculiar to each State" in the Union.[7]

After Willey's speech, the memorial for West Virginia statehood was referred to the Committee on Territories, chaired by Senator Wade, and was almost certain to include an antislavery provision when it came out of the committee.[8] The bill that the committee reported on June 26, 1862, required that West Virginians before admission to statehood must provide for the freedom of all black children born after July 4, 1863, and all other slaves when they reached their twenty-fifth birthday. It also expanded the area of the new state to include fifteen counties in the Shenandoah Valley, most of which had supported Virginia's secession in 1861.

Virginia senator Carlile, who had vigorously backed statehood, just as vigorously opposed the antislavery requirement. He was joined by Republicans Orville Browning and Jacob Collamer, who argued on constitutional grounds against Congress placing any restrictions on the admission of a new state. On the other hand, Charles Sumner, as expected, sought an immediate emancipation requirement for the new state. Senator Willey, fearful that statehood would not be approved, offered a substitute for the Wade committee's bill that would require gradual emancipation but not before admission to the Union. In addition to freeing black people born after July 1, 1863, and all other slaves after they reached twenty-five, the final Senate bill required a referendum on the question before statehood could be approved by Congress. The bill then passed the Senate on July 14 by a vote of 23 to 17, with all but one Northern Democrat and all border state conservatives voting against it, mainly because of its emancipation provision.[9]

Supporters of West Virginia statehood faced a more difficult task in the House of Representatives, where the question was not considered until July 16, the day before Congress adjourned. Republican Roscoe Conkling of New York made a motion to postpone the issue until Congress met in its third session in December. Although a number of Republican and (western) Virginia representatives opposed the motion because they believed that postponement would kill the statehood bill, it passed by a vote of 63 to 53.[10] When Congress reconvened, Republicans were more united than before on a bill requiring emancipation for the new state. They were probably influenced by Lincoln's promise to issue a proclamation on January 1 freeing slaves in the rebel states. Yet when consideration of the bill began on December 9, no word had come from the White House as to whether the president would sign it. Congress, however, moved forward with a brief debate on the West Virginia bill, and on December 10, the House by a vote of 96 to 55 joined the Senate in approving it.

After the West Virginia statehood bill was engrossed, Senator Browning took it to Lincoln on December 15. Browning recorded in his diary that the president "was deeply distressed at its passage, and asked me how long he could retain it before approving or vetoing [it]." When the senator told him ten days, Lincoln said that "he wished he had more" time. Browning replied that he "would give him a few days more" and said that he "would not lay it before him, but would retain it and furnish him a copy to examine."[11] The president questioned both the constitutional legitimacy, especially the irregular way in which the rump Virginia legislature had initiated the process, and the political expediency of the statehood bill.

Lincoln, however, was reluctant to veto a bill that was not central to the administration's prosecution of the war, and one that almost all his party's members in Congress had approved. Furthermore, the president did not desire to disappoint Governor Pierpont and other western Virginians who pleaded with him to sign the measure. From Wheeling, Pierpont telegraphed Lincoln on December 18 that a veto of the bill "would be disastrous to the cause in Western Virginia." Two days later, having learned that the president had not signed the bill, Pierpont again telegraphed him, declaring that the people in western Virginia "regard your delay as a calamity to the Union cause" and should be immediately set right.[12] The fact that the bill required gradual emancipation, though not compensation as Lincoln desired, also entered into his consideration of it. After all, the president was about to proclaim emancipation in the rebel states, and an antislavery requirement for West Virginia could advance the cause of freedom in the border states and reduce any charge of hypocrisy against him on the slavery issue.

The president thought that he needed the views of his cabinet members on the issue before making a decision. On December 23, he asked them to give their "opinion in writing" on whether they thought the statehood bill was "constitutional" and "expedient."[13] Six members wrote long responses, with Chase, Seward, and Stanton avowing both its constitutionality and expediency in support of western Virginia Unionists. Welles, Blair, and Bates doubted its efficacy. Bates, the attorney general, went further; he considered the whole "proceeding revolutionary" and probably wrongly advised Lincoln that Congress "will be glad to be relieved by a veto, from the evil consequences of such [an] improvident legislation."[14] This was not the only time that the attorney general's ultraconservatism would influence his judgment and advice to the president.

Reinforced by the support of his most important cabinet members for West Virginia statehood, the president signed the bill on December 31, one day before he issued his Emancipation Proclamation freeing slaves in the rebel states. West Virginia approved the conditions set by Congress for statehood, which included gradual emancipation, and on June 20, 1863, it entered the Union as a new state. On February 3, 1865, three days after Congress passed the Thirteenth Amendment and sent it to the states for ratification, the new West Virginia legislature provided for the immediate emancipation of all slaves in the state.[15]

In December 1861, Congress had appointed a special committee, the Joint Committee on the Conduct of the War (hereafter referred to as the War Committee), to guide the Lincoln administration on war policy, investigate military failures, and seek the removal of incompetent and failed military commanders. It also was charged with ferreting out corruption in military procurement and investigating abuses of prisoners of war by the rebels.

Although it had an innocuous beginning, the War Committee became a burr under Lincoln's saddle blanket, at times interfering in a harmful way with the administration's management of the conflict. Despite their assertion of knowledge about military affairs, Republican members of the committee could never understand the technical aspects of warfare and why generals could not always launch offensive actions. Historian Bruce Tap, the leading authority on the committee, has written that the result of the committee's interference "spawned distrust and jealousies among the top Union military commanders, helped undermine bipartisan support for the war, increased popular misconceptions about the nature of warfare, and contributed to the politicization of military appointments."[16] When Republican senator Lafayette Foster of Connecticut objected to any investigation of the army, Senator Fessenden, though not a member of the committee, replied that Congress's duty required it to determine how army appropriations were spent, including the investigation of military failures.[17]

The War Committee consisted of five Republicans and two Democrats. Chaired by "Bluff Ben" Wade, the committee was dominated by its Radical Republican members, who, from the beginning, had little confidence in President Lincoln's leadership or in generals like McClellan and Buell. In January and February 1862, the War Committee made several visits to the White House to urge the president to reorganize the army and replace McClellan in order to promote greater military efficiency. Lincoln refused to make the changes, explaining that he "dreaded the moral effect" of McClellan's removal, since the general, who had legions of supporters, would resign his command of the army. George W. Julian, a member of the committee, was especially appalled by the committee's first meeting with Lincoln in January. He wrote that "the most striking fact revealed by the discussion" with Lincoln "was that neither the president nor his advisors seemed to have any definite information respecting the management of the war, or the failure of our forces" under McClellan "to make any forward movement." The committee members, Julian reported, "were greatly surprised to learn that Mr. Lincoln himself did not think he had any *right* to know" about the general's plans.[18]

On another occasion, Senator Wade and a group of colleagues, probably members of his committee, called at the White House to protest the conduct of the war. After listening to Wade's complaint, Lincoln responded, "Senator, that reminds me of a story." Wade immediately cut him off and reportedly blurted out, "Bother your stories, Mr. President. That is the way it is with you sir. It is all story,

story. You are the father of every military blunder that has been made during the war. You are on the road to h———l, sir, with this Government, and you are not a mile off this minute." Unruffled, Lincoln calmly responded, "Wade, that is about the distance from here to the Capitol."[19]

Wade never warmed to Lincoln. On leaving the White House in early 1865, after the president rejected his advice to pursue a harsh reconstruction policy toward the South, the Ohio senator turned to a colleague and exclaimed, "Lincoln is a damned fool! He has no spirit, and [is] as weak as an old woman." Wade said that he would not be surprised if Lincoln, after the war, "fill[ed] the public offices with a horde of these infernal rebels."[20]

When Union military setbacks multiplied, Wade's War Committee increasingly irritated Lincoln. Yet the president never challenged the committee's right to investigate or criticize the administration, which reflected his "political education" to respect legislative committees and authority. Lincoln even refused to intervene when the War Committee went too far in its witch-hunting campaign against conservative generals who had failed or were openly hostile to the Republicans. General McClellan and his subordinates continued to be the special targets of the committee. Senator Zachariah Chandler of Michigan proved especially suspicious of officers educated at West Point. He divulged to a friend, "Lincoln means well, but has no force of character. He is surrounded by old Fogey Army officers more than one half of whom are down right traitors & ½ of the other half sympathize with the South."[21]

Hardly had the War Committee begun its work in 1862 when it launched an investigation into the army's defeat at Ball's Bluff on the Potomac River on October 21, 1861. Although blame for the disaster could be attributed to more than one officer, the War Committee, seeking a scapegoat, focused its attention on General Charles P. Stone, who commanded a division in the small battle near Washington. Based largely on hearsay evidence that Stone sympathized with the Confederates, the committee had him arrested and imprisoned for six months. Probably influenced by the fact that his close friend and U.S. senator, Colonel Edward D. Baker, had been killed in the battle, Lincoln refused to prevent this flagrant miscarriage of justice against an officer under his command.[22]

Another egregious case of injustice against an army officer was that of General Fitz John Porter, McClellan's second in command and an able officer by many accounts. Even Lincoln reportedly had praised Porter's skill in battle.[23] In late June, the eastern forces were reorganized, with Porter joining General John Pope's Army of Virginia. In the Battle of Second Bull Run in August 1862, General Lee's Army of Northern Virginia trounced Pope's forces. Outraged by another defeat, the Republicans on the War Committee and Secretary of War Edwin M. Stanton accepted Pope's claim that General Porter, a Democrat, had disobeyed orders and "shamefully" retreated from the advancing enemy forces in the battle, which constituted a high military offense.[24]

On November 12, 1862, Stanton formed a military commission to try Porter on the charges and stacked it against the general. The charges shocked Porter and his friends, including General McClellan, who insisted that not only was Porter blameless for the Bull Run defeat, but also his actions had actually saved the army from destruction in the battle. General Porter's defenders insisted that political motivation and General Pope's desire to cast blame elsewhere were the real reasons for the court-martial.[25]

In January 1863, members of the military commission brought in the verdict on Porter that Stanton and the War Committee wanted. They found him guilty of failure to obey his commander's orders at Bull Run and deliberately negligent in not sending detachments to aid the main army. The commission ordered General Porter "to be cashiered and to be forever disqualified from holding any office . . . in the government of the United States." After a perfunctory review of the case, the president, influenced by Judge Advocate General Joseph Holt's skewing of the evidence against Porter, approved the verdict.[26] In 1886, a military board of inquiry cleared Porter of blame and put his name back on the army rolls with the rank of colonel. The next day, having been vindicated, Porter resigned from the army.

When Congress returned in December 1862, Republicans were in an angry mood and worried about the future of the republic. The war continued to go badly, and their party, which they referred to as the Union Party, had suffered losses in the fall elections. Taking their cue from the War Committee, most Republicans believed that the failures of the military commanders to take vigorous action against the rebels could be attributed to their Democratic Party, if not outright disloyal, sentiments. However, the root of the problem, many Republicans concluded, was in the administration itself, specifically the overweening influence of Secretary of State William H. Seward and the president's reluctance to consult his cabinet on a regular basis. Both had resulted in a lack of harmony and a serious weakness in prosecuting the war, Republicans in Congress believed.

Republican opposition to Seward began as early as January 1861, when he advocated a compromise with the Southern secessionists, and it increased when he sought to become the premier of the government early in the war. Furthermore, the secretary's role in unilaterally suppressing civil liberties in 1861–62, his presumed interference in military operations, and his conduct of foreign affairs reportedly without the approval of the president did not sit well with Republicans in Congress. Fessenden expressed the opinion of many senators on both sides of the aisle when he wrote a friend at this time that Seward was "a poor creature—utterly selfish, false and mean." We are "getting fairly to detest him," Fessenden said.[27]

Overwhelmingly, Republican members wanted Seward out of the cabinet, though some also desired the dismissal of the antiradical thunderbolt Montgomery Blair and "old fossil" Edward Bates. The effort to get rid of Seward and reshape the administration climaxed in December 1862. Historians have usually told the story from the standpoint of the administration and have dismissed congressional concerns as a plot of the radicals to control the president and the war. Reportedly, radicals mainly were encouraged by the underhanded complaints of the ambitious Secretary of the Treasury Salmon P. Chase.

In their treatment of the affair, historians have probably been influenced by the biased antiradical accounts in the diaries of cabinet members Gideon Welles and Edward Bates and also Senator Orville Browning.[28] They have rightly applauded Lincoln's skillful handling of the resignations of Seward and Chase during the crisis.

However, historians have usually given too little attention or credit to the legitimate concerns of Senate Republicans and their attempts to arrive at a reasonable accommodation with the president regarding their concerns. Actually, Republicans of all factions (radicals, moderates, and conservatives) wanted changes in the administration and a greater commitment to a more vigorous prosecution of the war. They included conservative Republicans James Doolittle, James Dixon, and Edgar Cowan and middle-of-the-road Republicans Ira Harris and Preston King of New York and Jacob Collamer of Vermont. Even Browning voted in the Senate Republican caucus for a committee to meet with the president and express their dissatisfaction about the conduct of the war and problems in the cabinet. Except for a few senators such as Ben Wade, the Republicans did not propose to control the war effort or even the president's cabinet appointments, once Seward had been dismissed.

Sparked by still another military setback, this one at Fredericksburg on December 13, 1862, Senate Republicans met in caucus three days later to consider how to proceed in view of the deteriorating war situation. In a manuscript written soon after the events, Senator Fessenden provided the fullest and best account of the Republican caucus proceedings and subsequent meeting with Lincoln.[29] Senator Morton S. Wilkinson of Minnesota opened the caucus by declaring that, as Fessenden reported, "the country was ruined and the cause was lost." The Minnesota radical declared that "the source of all our difficulties and disasters was apparent," namely Secretary of State Seward, who "exercised a controlling influence upon the mind of the President. [Seward] never believed in the war," Wilkinson unfairly charged, "and so long as he remained in the Cabinet nothing but defeat and disaster could be expected."[30]

Senator Lafayette Foster of Connecticut disputed Wilkinson's claim that the war was lost, though he did agree with him that "no improvement could be expected in our affairs as long as Mr. Seward remained in the Cabinet." Others spoke in a similar vein. Senator Wade went further; he censured the president "for placing our armies under the command of officers who did not believe in the policy of the government and had no sympathy with its purposes."

Senator Collamer declared that "the difficulty was to be found in the fact that the President had no Cabinet in the true sense of the word." Collamer explained, "It was notorious that the President did not consult his Cabinet councilors, as a body, upon important matters." The Vermont senator indicated that he "had understood the President to have expressed the opinion that it was best to have no policy, and let each member of the Cabinet attend to the duties of his own department." Collamer thought that "measures should be taken to bring about a different state of things."[31]

Senator Fessenden then announced that "a crisis had arrived when [the Senate's] duty required an active interposition" in affairs. He wisely warned, however, that the Senate (he specifically meant the Republican caucus) "should proceed cautiously and with unanimity or its action would alarm the country and weaken the hand of the Executive without effecting any ultimate good. . . . At all events, [he] had no doubt that measures should be taken to make the Cabinet a unity and remove from it any one who did not coincide heartily with our views in relation to the war." Several senators wanted a resolution to that effect, but without mentioning the name of any cabinet member for dismissal. Senator Doolittle stated that instead of a resolution, a committee should be appointed to speak to the president regarding their concerns. Senator Preston King, a friend of Seward's, agreed. Fessenden doubted that the caucus could reach an agreement on a "definite proposition" to give to the president, and both Browning and Cowan wanted more time to consider the matter. With the senators unable to reach a decision, they adjourned to meet the next day.[32]

When the Republican caucus reconvened, Senator Ira Harris of New York offered a resolution, amended by Sumner, "that a committee be appointed to wait upon the President in behalf of senators here present and urge upon him changes in conduct and in the Cabinet which shall give the administration unity and vigor." The resolution was further amended by Fessenden to include "by a change in and partial reconstruction of the Cabinet." Although Senator John Sherman of Ohio announced his intention to support the resolution, he seized the opportunity to attack Lincoln. "The difficulty was with the

President himself," he asserted. Lincoln, the Ohio senator claimed, "had neither dignity, order, nor firmness." Sherman preferred "to go directly to the President himself, and tell him his defects. It was doubtful if even that would do any good." The Harris resolution passed by a unanimous vote, but with Senator King not voting. The Republican caucus chose a committee of nine senators, chaired by Collamer, to meet with the president.[33]

The next day, Senator Collamer sent a note to Lincoln requesting an interview; the president replied that he would meet with the caucus committee that evening. Before the meeting, Collamer prepared a brief paper "embodying the views of the Republican members of the Senate, as he understood them." The paper, which the committee agreed to, concluded by expressing "the most unqualified confidence in the patriotism and integrity of the President, identified as they are with the success of his administration, [and] profoundly impressed with the critical condition of our national affairs." The Republican senators were "deeply convinced that the public confidence requires a practical regard to [their] propositions and principles . . . for executive consideration and action."[34]

Senator King immediately reported to Secretary of State Seward about the forthcoming meeting. Shaken by the news, Seward just as quickly submitted his resignation to the president. On December 18, Senator Browning, having gone with a friend to see Lincoln on another matter, was called back by the president as he was leaving the office. Browning wrote in his diary, "He asked me if I was at the caucus yesterday." When the senator replied that he was at the meeting, Lincoln, who seemed deeply distressed, asked his friend, "What do these men want?" Browning, according to his account, answered, "I hardly know Mr President, but they are exceedingly violent towards the administration, and what we did yesterday was the gentlest thing that could be done." Whereupon Lincoln said, "They wish to get rid of me, and I am sometimes half disposed to gratify them."[35]

Browning quickly realized that he had misled the president into believing the worst and that all the Republican senators opposed him. He told Lincoln, "Some of them do wish to get rid of you, but the fortunes of the Country are bound up with your fortunes, and you [must] stand firmly at your post and hold the helm with a steady hand—To relinquish it now would bring upon us certain and inevitable ruin." Without acknowledging his friend's reassurance, Lincoln dejectedly remarked, probably with the Fredericksburg defeat in mind, "We are now on the brink of destruction. It appears to me the Almighty is against us, and I can hardly see a ray of hope." Browning assured him that Seward, not the president, was the real object of "the ultra, impracticable men," which did little to improve his mood. Then, referring to the charges against Seward, Lincoln sadly commented, "Why will men believe a lie, an absurd lie, that [they] could not impose upon a child, and cling to it and repeat it in defiance of all evidence to the contrary." Browning did not respond. In bidding his friend good night, Lincoln revealed, "Since I heard last night of the proceedings of the caucus, I have been more distressed than by any event of my life."[36]

When the committee of the Republican caucus met with the president in the White House on December 18, Senator Collamer began by reading his brief paper outlining the views of the caucus. When he had finished, and without elaborating, the Vermont senator relinquished the floor to other members of the committee for their opinions. Ben Wade rose and criticized the president for leaving the war in the hands of commanders who had no sympathy for the cause. He spoke at length on the recent elections in the West, imputing the defeat of the Union Party there, according to Fessenden, "to the fact that the President had placed the direction of our military affairs in the hands of bitter and malignant Democrats."[37]

Other senators in the meeting agreed. Fessenden told Lincoln that "it was singularly unfortunate that almost every officer known as an anti-slavery man had been disgraced" and that "largely pro-slavery and men [who] sympathized strongly with the Southern feeling" had been retained. The senators also expressed concern that the president had neglected to consult his cabinet on important matters relating to the war. Along this line, Fessenden claimed that Seward "was not in accord with the majority of the Cabinet and exerted an injurious influence upon the conduct of the war." Fessenden, however, informed Lincoln that it was not the purpose of the Republican senators "to dictate to him with regard to his Cabinet." Nonetheless, the importance of the emergency in national affairs, he said, rendered it necessary for the president to consult frequently with all "his constitutional advisers [for] their friendly counsel."[38]

Senator Sumner then launched into a bitter attack on Seward's conduct of foreign affairs. He claimed that the secretary of state "had subjected himself to ridicule in diplomatic circles at home and abroad." Furthermore, Sumner declared, Seward "had uttered statements offensive to Congress and spoken of it repeatedly with disrespect in the presence of foreign ministers." On one occasion, Sumner charged, the secretary had sent a dispatch that placed the rebels and the majority in Congress "upon the same levels." He did not indicate the occasion. According to the Massachusetts senator, Seward also "had written offensive dispatches which the President could not have seen or assented to."[39]

After three hours, the meeting ended, but without any agreement or action to be taken. The next day, December 19, the president asked for another session with the committee, which occurred that evening. Before the meeting, Lincoln met with members of the cabinet, except Seward, and requested that they join him in the discussion with the Senate Republican committee. Chase protested and announced that until he entered the room, he knew nothing of the Republican caucus movement or Seward's resignation. He perhaps protested too much, since in his designing way the Treasury secretary often complained to Republicans in Congress about the lack of leadership in the administration, including the president's reluctance to pursue a vigorous antislavery policy. However, Chase agreed, along with the other cabinet members and the president, to meet with Collamer and the senators that evening.[40] Lincoln did not invite Seward to join the group.

When the members of the Republican committee arrived at the White House, they were surprised to find the cabinet, except for Seward, assembled in the anteroom. Lincoln asked them if they had any objection to having the cabinet present "for a free and friendly conversation" on the issues relating to the cabinet that had been discussed in the first meeting. No one objected, whereupon the president, according to Senator Fessenden, "opened with a speech, admitting that the Cabinet had not been very regular in its consultations, but excusing it for want of time." He said that "most questions of importance had received a reasonable consideration," and he "was not aware of any divisions or want of unity" in the cabinet.[41]

Fessenden found it "remarkable that in the course of his speech, which was quite long," the president acknowledged "several instances in which most important action" was taken "not only without consultation with his Cabinet, but without the knowledge of several [members]." These included his reinstatement of McClellan as commander of the army in Virginia and General Henry W. Halleck as general in chief. Lincoln defended Seward's role in the administration, insisting that he "had been earnest in the prosecution of the war, and had not improperly interfered" with the management of the other departments. Indeed, Lincoln said, Seward had sometimes consulted with Chase on matters relating to foreign affairs. Despite claims to the contrary, the president reported that Seward "had generally read him his official correspondence" before sending it.[42]

After Lincoln had concluded his remarks, he asked members of his cabinet to say whether there had been any lack of unity or insufficient consultation with them. Realizing that he had been placed in an untenable situation, and not wanting to suggest that he had been underhanded and disloyal to the administration, Chase endorsed the president's statement "fully and entirely," according to Secretary of the Navy Welles. However, Chase indicated, he "regretted that there was not a more full and thorough consideration and canvass of all important measures in open cabinet."[43]

Two other cabinet members, Montgomery Blair and Edward Bates, endorsed Lincoln's position and declared that the president, as Blair insisted, "was accountable for his administration,—might ask opinions or not" of cabinet members. Blair and Bates admitted that they had had differences with Seward, but they believed that he should not be dismissed from the cabinet. Welles and Secretary of War Stanton remained silent, though the secretary of the navy expressed his sentiments in his diary. Welles wrote, "A senatorial combination to dictate to the President in regard to his political family in the height of a civil war which threatens the existence of the republic cannot be permitted, even if the person [Seward] to whom they object is as obnoxious as they represent."[44]

The senators in the meeting then largely repeated their criticism of Seward and the lack of consultation in the administration, though Senator Harris of New York said that the removal of Seward would be "calamitous" in his state. In addition to making several speeches during the meeting, Lincoln, to the irritation of Fessenden, "related several anecdotes, most of which," the senator wrote, "I had heard before."[45] Although storytelling was a habit with Lincoln and provided some relief from his toils, the serious nature of the meeting hardly made it a proper occasion for his anecdotes. Nonetheless, the president, as he did on other occasions, handled the Republican Senate leadership with considerable tact and thoughtfulness.

After more than five hours of discussion, the meeting adjourned. Most of the committee members left the White House disappointed that the president did not at least indicate he would accept Seward's resignation. Browning, who was not on the committee, later asked its chairman, Senator Collamer, how Chase could say to the senators that the cabinet had been harmonious when he had earlier reported to them that Seward "exercised a back stair and malign influence upon the President and thwarted all the measures of the Cabinet." Collamer answered, "He lied."[46] Despite the belief of Browning, several cabinet members, and even Lincoln, the Republican caucus, as Fessenden insisted, did not seek to dominate the administration. Although they sought the removal of Seward, the senators wanted mainly to make the president aware of the dissension in the administration and the need for him to consult with his cabinet on a regular basis. They also recommended that all important public measures be taken and appointments be made only after the approval of a majority of the cabinet.

The Republican senators inadvertently had done Lincoln a favor by raising the issue of discord in the cabinet. The day after the meeting, Chase arrived at the White House with a letter of resignation in hand. This provided the president with the opportunity to pair it with Seward's letter and end the cabinet crisis by refusing the resignations of both ministers. In the presence of Welles, Lincoln grabbed the letter from Chase, who seemed reluctant to give it up, and, looking toward the navy secretary, he gave "a triumphant laugh" and announced that it "cuts the gordian not [*sic*]" in the affair. "My way is clear—the trouble is ended," he declared. The president could not afford politically to accept either resignation. Lincoln told Browning, "with a good deal of emphasis," that he now "was master" of his administration.[47]

At the same time, the crisis had largely cleared the air between the president and his party's leaders in Congress. Both realized that cooperation between the executive and legislative branches to save the Union were too important for a schism to occur in their relationship. Despite differences (for example, on the confiscation of rebel property) and the fact that many Republicans had little faith in Lincoln's leadership, they never again attempted to dictate to him regarding control of his administration. After the failure to remove Seward, one erstwhile radical, Representative Henry Dawes of Massachusetts, disgustedly wrote to his wife, Electra, "The President is an imbecile and should be sent to the school for feeble minded youth. . . . Meanwhile the poor country is going to perdition as fast as possible."[48]

On December 1, 1862, the president sent Congress his annual message reporting on the state of affairs and recommending legislation for its consideration. He began by summarizing and commenting on the reports of the various departments. He admitted that foreign affairs, especially with the British, had been troubled during the year as a result of "the temporary reverses which befell the national arms, and which were exaggerated by our own disloyal citizens [rebels] abroad." Lincoln astutely observed, "Our struggle has been, of course, contemplated by foreign nations with reference less to its own merits, than to its supposed, and often exaggerated effects and consequences resulting to those nations themselves. Nevertheless, complaint on the part of this government, even if it were just, would certainly be unwise" as long as the nation struggled for its survival. The president did happily report success in negotiating a treaty with Great Britain to suppress the slave trade while preserving "a jealous respect for the authority of the United States."[49]

Lincoln simply transmitted the reports of the secretaries of war and the navy to Congress without comment. He provided a summary of the secretary of the interior's report that focused on Indian affairs and announced that "the Indian tribes upon our frontiers have, during the past year, manifested a spirit of insubordination, and, at several points, have engaged in open hostilities against the white settlements in their vicinity." He specifically referred to the "wholly unexpected" Sioux uprising in Minnesota in which settlements were attacked "with extreme ferocity, killing, indiscriminately, men, women, and children." Lincoln admitted that he did not know "how this outbreak was induced." However, he told Congress, "I submit for your especial consideration whether our Indian system shall not be remodeled. Many wise and good men have impressed me with the belief that this can be profitably done."[50]

The only action on the Indian issue that the Thirty-Seventh Congress took during its 1862–63 session was to authorize the administration to negotiate removal treaties with the tribes. In his next annual message, on December 8, 1863, the president reported that "stipulations for extinguishing the possessory rights of the Indians to large and valuable tracts of land" had been made. At the same time, he reminded Congress of the "urgent need for immediate legislative action" on Indian reform.[51]

In his December 1, 1862, annual message on federal finances, Lincoln provided Congress with an extensive summary of Secretary of the Treasury Chase's report. The president applauded "the judicious legislation of Congress" in authorizing the issuance of greenbacks and making them legal tender for debts and internal duties, which provided "partially, at least for the time, the long felt want of a uniform circulating medium." He said, however, that "a return to specie payments . . . should ever be kept in view." As before, Lincoln called on Congress to give its "most diligent consideration" to appropriating "the necessary revenue, without injury to business and with the least possible burdens upon labor," to fight the war.[52]

The president devoted the last part of his 1862 annual message to his emancipation efforts during the year and his support for black colonization as a solution to racial conflict and other social problems

following the end of slavery. He surprisingly proposed three constitutional amendments to further both emancipation and colonization.
In introducing the proposed amendments, Lincoln called Congress's
attention to the second paragraph in his September 22 preliminary
Emancipation Proclamation. In it, Lincoln had promised that at
Congress's next meeting, he would "again recommend the adoption
of a practical measure tendering pecuniary aid to the free acceptance
or rejection of all slave states" not in rebellion and that "may then have
voluntarily adopted, or thereafter may voluntarily adopt, immediate
or gradual abolishment of slavery." The September 22 proclamation
also included his promise to continue "the effort to colonize persons
of African descent, with their consent, upon this continent, or elsewhere," contingent on the approval of the foreign governments.[53]

As indicated above, Lincoln proposed three articles to amend
the Constitution. In the first article, he outlined a procedure for the
delivery and payment of federal bonds to cooperating states for the
immediate or gradual emancipation of the slaves. The article failed to
specify the amount to be distributed to the slaveholders, except that it
should be based on an aggregate sum for the slaves listed in the 1860
census. The process of emancipation in a state need not be completed
until 1900. The second article provided that "all slaves who shall have
enjoyed actual freedom by the chances of the war, at any time before
the end of the rebellion, shall be forever free; but all owners of such,
who shall not have been disloyal, shall be compensated for them." The
third article read, "Congress may appropriate money, and otherwise
provide, for colonizing free colored persons, with their own consent,
at any place or places without the United States."[54]

Lincoln predicted that if the amendments were adopted, "emancipation will follow, at least, in several of the States." The policy of gradual
emancipation, which he preferred, "spares both races from the evils
of sudden derangement." Some antislavery supporters, Lincoln said,
"will deprecate the length of time" since "it gives too little to the now
living slaves. But it really gives them much," he argued, because "it
saves them from the vagrant destitution which must largely attend
immediate emancipation in localities where their numbers are very
great." In addition, "the plan leaves to each State" its acceptance and

implementation, including the mode of compensation. White people "whose habitual course of thought will be disturbed by the measure will have passed away before its consummation. They will never see it."[55]

The president suggested that the third article calling for Congress to appropriate money for voluntary black colonization was designed to lessen the growing fear among Northerners that their communities would be overrun by freed slaves and white labor would be depressed. Although unstated, Lincoln believed that he had to have the support of conservative Republicans, border state Unionists, and Northern Democrats for his emancipation proposal to succeed. He maintained that colonization, though voluntary and probably limited at first, would go far toward alleviating the white fear of black freedom. Lincoln admitted, "There is an objection urged against free colored persons remaining in the country, which is largely imaginary, if not sometimes malicious." Under no circumstances did he believe that "the freed people will swarm forth, and cover the whole land." They will probably "stay in their old places [and] jostle no white laborers."[56]

Lincoln's proposed constitutional amendments provided the back-drop for his historic admonition in his annual message for Congress to approve and send the articles to the states for ratification. "The dogmas of the quiet past are inadequate to the stormy present," he told the legislators. "The occasion is piled high with difficulty, and we must rise with the occasion. As our case is new, so we must think anew, and act anew. Fellow-citizens, *we* cannot escape history. We of this Congress and this administration, will be remembered in spite of ourselves. . . . The fiery trial through which we pass, will light us down, in honor or dishonor, to the latest generation." He went on, "We *say* we are for the Union. . . . We know how to save the Union. . . . In *giving* freedom to the *slave,* we *assure* freedom to the *free*—honorable alike in what we give, and what we preserve. We shall nobly save, or meanly lose, the last best, hope of earth. Other means may succeed; this could not fail. The way is plain, peaceful, generous, just—a way which, if followed, the world will forever applaud, and God must forever bless."[57]

Observers inside and outside of Congress quickly recognized that Lincoln's emancipation and colonization proposal was a "grand illu-sion" on his part, as abolitionist William Lloyd Garrison characterized it. They could see that the three amendments, even if they could achieve Lincoln's objectives, could not be approved by the required two-thirds of Congress and ratified by three-fourths of the states within a reasonable period of time. Senator Browning predicted that the process, even if no opposition existed, would take four years to approve.[58] Although some Republican congressmen gave Lincoln credit for his good intentions to end slavery, others, especially radicals, denounced the proposal. Representative Henry Winter Davis of Maryland, who also had other issues with the president, declared, "There are some, and the President is among them, who labor under the delusion that you can free the Negroes and send them off to a foreign land. The thing is an impossibility; and if it were practicable, it would not be desirable."[59] Although Lincoln backed a resettlement venture on an island off Haiti, it collapsed in near disaster in 1863, and he did not again actively support colonization.

Lincoln soon gave up on the attempt to secure congressional action on his proposed constitutional amendments. However, he continued to lobby border state congressmen to urge their states to approve his compensation plan for ending slavery. In December, the president met with Senator John B. Henderson of Missouri, who agreed to introduce a bill in the Senate that would provide $20 million for the implementation of the plan in his state. Representative John W. Noell of Missouri anticipated Henderson's move by introducing a similar bill in the House of Representatives. Although an amended bill passed the Senate, the effort went awry in the House, where a coalition of border state Unionists and Northern Democrats secured the bill's defeat, ostensibly over the amount to be paid for each freed slave and the deadline for the completion of emancipation.[60]

In early 1863, Congress turned its attention to the critical manpower needs of the army after the staggering losses of 1862, including tens of thousands of desertions. The growing resistance to the war, especially in the lower North, and the increasing dissatisfaction with the Republican leadership also created a new sense of urgency for Congress, the president, and the War Department. Secretary of War Stanton, who complained of "serious defects" in the militia law, worked with Henry Wilson, chairman of the Senate Committee on Military Affairs, to draft a national conscription bill to raise troops. Stanton's recent biographer has questioned whether the secretary of war even brought Lincoln deeply into the discussions on the bill.[61]

On February 9, after consideration by his committee, Wilson introduced the conscription bill in the Senate. A similar bill was introduced in the House of Representatives on February 23. In both chambers, intense debate broke out over the measure for "enrolling and calling out the national forces."[62] A military draft would follow at the call of the War Department for troops. Opposition in Congress could be heard from conservatives and Democrats, who vehemently insisted that the bill was unconstitutional in that it violated the rights of the states to raise military forces, and it also treaded on the liberties of the people. In the House, Democrat John B. Steele of New York, whose brother Frederick would soon command Union forces in Arkansas, issued a blistering attack on the enrollment bill. Steele particularly objected to the proposed legislation because it was "one of a series of measures which centralize power in the Federal Government" at the expense of the states and local governments. He took sharp exception to Thaddeus Stevens's reference to Democrats as "rebel sympathizers and traitors," attributing the remark of the Pennsylvania radical to his "imbittered [sic] malice of impotent hate." Steele charged that Stevens sought "to take advantage of the country's distresses to urge the accomplishment of mad schemes, to the imminent peril of the national existence."[63] Stevens ignored what he considered a pop-gun attack by a Copperhead.

Democrats also denounced the provision for the appointment of federal provost marshals throughout the country to enforce the enrollment of men eligible for the draft, those who were physically able and between the ages of twenty and forty-five. Representative George Pendleton, who would be the Democratic candidate for vice president in 1864, severely criticized the president's control of the marshals as dangerous to civil liberties. He asked, "What imperial power is this? What autocrat has ever more" power than under this law?[64]

A number of congressmen, including Republicans, questioned a provision permitting men who were drafted to hire a substitute or pay as much as a $300 commutation fee, though the War Department could determine a lower amount. Senator Wilson weakly argued that the commutation fee would eliminate the corrupt bonus system for hiring recruits. The commutation provision left the bill's Republican supporters subject to the charge that it was "a rich man's war, but a poor man's fight." Senator Trumbull recognized the problem for his party in Illinois when he replied to Wilson that the commutation fee, even if set low, was "not a provision in favor of the poor men of the country. They cannot buy the right to stay at home."[65] An effort to get rid of the commutation clause, however, failed in the Senate by a partisan vote. In the House, although the provision was retained, 29 of the 95 Republicans who were present and voting joined the Democrats to eliminate it.[66]

A controversy over the recruitment of black troops seriously complicated the passage of the conscription bill. In the Emancipation Proclamation on January 1, 1863, President Lincoln had finally authorized black troops in the military, though at first for garrison duty only. On January 12, Stevens introduced a bill in the House of Representatives to recruit 150,000 black troops. The proposal immediately ran into a storm of protest from border state Unionists and Northern Democrats. Orville Browning, who had recently been replaced in the Senate, predicted that if Stevens's bill passed, they would "lose Ky, Tennessee, Maryland and Missouri" and "a restoration of the Union will no longer be possible."[67] After an amendment designed to satisfy conservatives, the black recruitment proposal passed the House by a strictly Republican vote, along with the enrollment or conscription bill.

But the recruitment measure became stalled in the Senate after Garret Davis of Kentucky offered an amendment barring black men from inclusion in the enrollment bill. By a vote of 23 to 12, the amendment failed to pass, whereupon on March 2, Davis's Kentucky colleague Lazarus W. Powell introduced a new amendment to the enrollment bill prohibiting the commissioning of any "person of African descent" as an officer in the army. Several conservative Republicans joined the Democrats and border state members in approving Powell's amendment. The enrollment bill, as amended, then passed the Senate, and the president signed it on March 3, 1863.[68] That same day, the Thirty-Seventh Congress adjourned for the last time.

The Thirty-Seventh Congress had achieved a remarkable record since convening on July 4, 1861, for its first session at President Lincoln's call. It had authorized the emergency actions that Lincoln had taken immediately after Fort Sumter and given him ample authority and resources to conduct the war. It had also passed the Crittenden-Johnson Resolutions approving the Union-only purpose of the war, thereby avoiding a conflict over slavery, which could have undermined support for the cause in the border states and among Northern Democrats and conservative Republicans.

When the Thirty-Seventh Congress met in December 1861 for its second session, the war had become hard, motivating fretful Republicans to take the initiative and pass legislation of lasting significance. In most cases, Lincoln readily signed the legislation. At least three of these measures had little direct relationship to the prosecution of the war, but they had received considerable support before the war, only to fail mainly because of the opposition of Democrats such as President James Buchanan. Backed by varying Northern and western interests, and not strictly along party lines, these measures were the Pacific Railway Act, Land-Grant College Act, and Homestead Act, all enacted during the summer of 1862.

This session of Congress also began the process of ending slavery in the United States. In April 1862, it abolished slavery in the District of Columbia, and in July, it passed the Second Confiscation Act, designed partly to free the slaves of rebels and use them in the army, even as soldiers. Lincoln signed the measures after Congress accepted some of his reservations. Congress agreed in principle to fund the president's proposal for gradual, compensated emancipation by the Union border states that would approve it. No state, however, accepted the plan.

The second session of the Thirty-Seventh Congress also created the Joint Committee on the Conduct of the War, a move that Lincoln did not like but did not resist. The committee was formed for the purpose of investigating and reporting on conditions related to the prosecution of the conflict, an assignment that it rigorously carried out in ways that were often biased against and unjust toward Democratic generals and detrimental to a unified military effort. The fact that Senator Ben Wade, a critic of the administration, chaired the committee became a source of tension between the president and the radicals on the committee.

The last session of the Thirty-Seventh Congress in early 1863 provided strong backing for Lincoln's Emancipation Proclamation and his authorization for the recruitment of black troops in the army. In addition, this session of Congress enacted the first federal military conscription bill in American history. The implementation of conscription, along with the suspension of the writ of habeas corpus, ensured that the bitter political divisions over the war and Republican policies would continue, especially as long as the Union battlefield situation did not improve. Despite its achievements, when the Thirty-Seventh Congress adjourned on March 3, military success for the Union seemed remote, with no end in sight for the troubles Lincoln and the Republicans faced. The new Congress would not convene until December.

William Pitt Fessenden, Republican senator of Maine and chairman of the Senate Finance Committee

Thaddeus Stevens, Radical Republican representative of Pennsylvania and chairman of the House Ways and Means Committee

Jacob Collamer, influential Republican senator of Vermont

Lyman Trumbull, Republican senator of Illinois and chairman of the
Senate Judiciary Committee

Charles Sumner, Radical Republican senator of Massachusetts and chairman of the Senate Foreign Affairs Committee

Henry Winter Davis, Radical Republican representative of Maryland, coauthor of the Wade-Davis reconstruction bill, and chairman of the House Foreign Affairs Committee

Samuel S. "Sunset" Cox, Democratic representative of Ohio and a minority leader in the House of
Representatives

John Jordan Crittenden, conservative senator and later representative of Kentucky, and coauthor of the Crittenden-Johnson Resolutions of July 1861 on the Union purpose in the war

James Mitchell Ashley, Republican representative of Ohio and leader of the successful effort in the House to secure the passage (initiation) of the Thirteenth Amendment

Orville H. Browning, conservative Republican senator of
Illinois and longtime friend of Lincoln

UNION RESURGENCE

Rampant discontent and defeatism plagued the Union states during the spring of 1863. This was especially true in the lower North. Copperheads had seized control of the Indiana and Illinois legislatures and had become a powerful force in Ohio and Pennsylvania. They were determined to consolidate their gains. In Indiana, Peace Democrats withdrew funding for the state Republican administration, whereupon Governor Oliver Perry Morton had to obtain War Department funds and donations to maintain his government and provide support for his state troops. The legislature of New Jersey, traditionally Democratic, passed a Copperhead resolution calling for an end to the war. However, Governor Joel Parker, while denouncing Lincoln's policies, continued to support the war. Likewise, Horatio Seymour, the new Democratic governor of New York, backed the war to suppress the rebellion but vigorously opposed the president and Republican congressional policies. These included emancipation, suspension of the writ of habeas corpus, military arrests, and conscription. Seymour's unrelenting and penetrating attacks on Lincoln and the Republicans provided grist for the Democratic mills in New York and elsewhere.

General Ambrose E. Burnside, the new commander of the Department of the Ohio, made matters worse for Lincoln and the Republicans when he issued General Order Number 38 on April 13, 1863, directing the military arrests of rebel sympathizers in his region. The arrest, military trial, and imprisonment of recent Ohio congressman and Copperhead leader Clement Vallandigham followed in May, creating a serious and unwanted problem for the president. Lincoln refused to repudiate Burnside's action, though he commuted "Prince Val's" sentence to exile in the Confederacy. Burnside's action alarmed many congressmen, including some Republicans, who nonetheless remained publicly silent. In New York, Democratic congressman Erastus Corning chaired a mass rally that adopted resolutions to be sent to Lincoln denouncing General Burnside's violations of constitutional liberties and demanding that the president act to prohibit military intervention in the Union states.

Lincoln replied in a carefully crafted public letter, known as the Corning letter, in which he defended military arrests and at the same time, he believed, would satisfy Northerners and border state Unionists who were troubled by the government's restrictions on civil liberties. He declared that the military arrests and trials were constitutionally correct, necessitated by the period of national crisis the United States was experiencing. Lincoln wrote that because of his "reverence for the guarranteed [sic] rights of individuals," he had been "slow to adopt strong measures" against violators who, he claimed, were "too numerous and powerful for the ordinary courts of justice." The arrests, the president insisted, had become "indispensable to the public Safety."[1]

The president's Corning letter garnered praise from Republicans, but not from Democrats including Seymour and those in the Copperhead faction of the party. For Democrats, Lincoln's justification for the suspension of the writ of habeas corpus and military arrests and trials confirmed in their minds the administration's determination to rule by military decree, in collaboration with the Republicans in Congress. This was not the intention of the president or the Republicans; their purpose in the military arrests was the suppression of "traitors" in the North who gave aid and comfort to the rebels by resisting conscription and other war measures. Nonetheless, as historian Mark E. Neely Jr. has written, "The Corning letter of Abraham Lincoln is the strongest statement ever made by any American president asserting the power of the government to restrict civil liberty."[2]

During July 1863, the battlefield situation took a dramatic turn in favor of the Union, providing renewed hope that victory could soon be achieved. At Gettysburg, Union troops under George G. Meade defeated General Robert E. Lee's army. Battered but still very much alive, the Confederate army retreated back to Virginia. In the western theater, General U. S. Grant forced the surrender of thirty thousand rebels at Vicksburg, thereby virtually opening the Mississippi River to the Union and dividing the Confederacy. These victories were briefly marred by violent opposition in the North to the first draft under the conscription law, with the worst rioting occurring in New York City in mid-July. In September, a Confederate victory at Chickamauga in North Georgia and the siege of federal forces at Chattanooga were reminders that hard fighting remained before the war could be won.

The off-year fall elections of 1863 heralded a revival of patriotic support for the war and for the Republicans. The Union Party victories in the lower North and New York also revealed that opposition to the Enrollment Act (conscription), in the wake of the army's successes, had ceased to be an issue that could stir passion and violence at the polls.[3] The commutation issue, however, continued to plague the president and Congress. When demands reached Lincoln to order an end to the enforcement of the commutation provision in the Enrollment Act, he replied that he had no authority to override the law. But on June 8, 1864, he obtained congressional repeal of the controversial clause. Although conscription probably secured the reenlistment of many volunteers who otherwise would have returned home, the number of men who were actually drafted fell far short of the objective of Congress and the War Department. Of the 2,667,999 men who donned the blue during the war, only 46,347 were forced to serve, and many of them proved to be poor soldiers.[4]

On December 7, 1863, the Thirty-Eighth Congress met for its first session. Despite the setbacks for Republicans in the 1862 elections, the party of Lincoln still possessed a fairly comfortable majority in both chambers, though Emerson Etheridge, the outgoing clerk and a renegade Unionist of Tennessee, unsuccessfully plotted to exclude regularly elected Republicans and place Democrats on the roll in the House of Representatives.[5] An almanac for 1864, although inexact, reported that 36 Republicans and "Unconditional Unionists" and 14

Democrats held seats in the Senate. In the House of Representatives, the almanac counted 102 Republicans and "Unconditional Unionists," 75 Democrats, and 9 "Border State Men."[6]

A brief contest occurred in the House over the speakership before Schuyler Colfax of Indiana, a congenial former newspaper editor, was elected. Although "Smiler" Colfax's political sentiments as a middle-of-the-road Republican were similar to Lincoln's, the president, according to Secretary of the Navy Welles, lacked "confidence in Colfax, whom he considers a little intriguer,—plausible but not trustworthy." Lincoln, however, as was his policy in congressional affairs, did not attempt to influence the election of the speaker.[7]

On December 9, 1863, Lincoln sent his annual message to Congress, where it was read by a clerk. As before, he summarized the reports of the department heads and gave his own conclusions, which were largely positive. He applauded the fact that "we remain in peace and friendship with foreign powers, [despite] the efforts of disloyal citizens of the United States to involve us in foreign wars, to aid an inexcusable insurrection." The president informed Congress, and by extension the American public, that a supplemental treaty with Great Britain, following earlier negotiations, had been ratified in February. This, he believed, had brought to an end the "inhuman and odious traffic" in slaves in America.[8]

Lincoln reported that "the operations of the treasury during the last year [had] been successfully conducted," and he provided figures to demonstrate his point. He announced that "the enactment by Congress of a national banking law" during the year had "proved a valuable support of the public credit" and loans. "All demands on the treasury, including the pay of the army and navy, have been promptly met and fully satisfied." He praised the American people, who had "cheerfully borne . . . the burdens incident to a great war."[9]

Without attempting a summary, the president referred Congress to the report of the secretary of war, which he characterized "as a document of great interest," and also to that of the secretary of the navy. He deferred comment on the war and reconstruction to the last part of his message. Lincoln called Congress's attention to the secretary of the interior's "useful and varied information in relation to the public lands, Indian affairs, patents, pensions, and other matters of public concern." He was particularly pleased to report that 1,456,049 acres of public land had been "taken up under the homestead law," for military bounties, and for railroad and other purposes. Lincoln reminded Congress that in the distribution of public lands (he referred to the land as being "disposed of"), the American people "had a higher and more enduring interest in the early settlement and substantial cultivation of [these] lands than in the amount of direct revenue to be derived from the sale of them. This opinion has had a controlling influence in shaping legislation upon the subject of our national domain."[10] Lincoln could not have anticipated that after the war, railroad and land companies would receive the lion's share of the public lands, not bona fide settlers as he had hoped.

The liberal public land policy of Lincoln and Congress did not extend to the western Indians. The president reported to Congress, "The measures provided at your last session for the removal of certain Indian tribes have been carried into effect." He indicated that treaties with "sundry tribes" had been negotiated, "which, in due time, will be submitted for the constitutional action of the Senate. They contain stipulations for extinguishing the possessory rights of the Indians to large and valuable tracts of land." He hoped "that the effect of these treaties will result in the establishment of permanent friendly relations with [the] tribes" that had been "brought into frequent and bloody collision with our outlying settlements and emigrants." Lincoln reminded Congress that in his last annual message, he had suggested "the propriety of remodeling our Indian system. Subsequent events have satisfied me of its necessity." He referred Congress to the secretary of the interior's report for the details of "the urgent need for immediate legislative action" on the issue.[11] Although Indian reform bills were introduced into the Senate and the House in this session of Congress, they failed to pass.

The president then reported that when Congress met one year earlier, the war for the Union had achieved "varying results." At that time, he said, "the rebellion had been pressed back into reduced limits; yet the tone of public feeling and opinion, at home and abroad, was not satisfactory," including "uneasiness among ourselves." Lincoln recalled that "amid much that was cold and menacing the kindest words coming from Europe were uttered in accents of pity, that we were too blind to surrender a hopeless cause." He bitterly noted that despite the protests of his administration, the Europeans had permitted armed vessels to be built and outfitted in their ports, and these vessels threatened to "sweep our trade from the sea and raise our blockade."[12]

Since then, Lincoln reported to Congress, the war had turned for the better. "The policy of emancipation, and of employing black soldiers," had given "to the future a new aspect" of hope. "So far as tested, it is difficult to say" that the black troops "are not as good soldiers as any." Furthermore, despite fears, "no servile insurrection, or tendency to violence or cruelty, has marked the measures of emancipation and arming the blacks." In addition, "the rebel borders" had been "pressed still further back, and by the complete opening of the Mississippi," the rebel country had been "divided into distinct parts, with no practical communication between them." Tennessee and Arkansas, he confidently announced, had been "substantially cleared of insurgent control, and influential citizens . . . now declare openly for emancipation."[13]

In view of these encouraging signs, Lincoln informed Congress that he had "thought fit to issue a proclamation" of amnesty and reconstruction (he preferred "restoration," meaning the restoration of loyal governments similar to those that he had initiated in Union-occupied Louisiana and was attempting in Tennessee). The reconstruction proclamation, which he issued on the same day as his message to Congress, required emancipation and had provisions for the education of young black people. He also required the participation of 10 percent of the 1860 voters in the restoration of civil government.[14]

In issuing his reconstruction proclamation, which became known as his Ten Percent Plan, Lincoln announced that as president he had the authority to grant amnesty and pardons to any persons transgressing against the Constitution and laws and also to restore republican forms of government in the rebellious states. The Ten Percent Plan provided that whenever one-tenth of the voters in any rebel state in the 1860 presidential election had taken the oath of allegiance and had not subsequently violated it, they could form a loyal government. Lincoln did not explain why the ten percent formula was chosen. He probably concluded that while the war raged, ten percent of the voters before secession would constitute a tangible nucleus to launch Union governments. He announced, "It may be proper to further say that whether members sent to Congress from any State shall be admitted to seats, constitutionally rests exclusively with the respective Houses, and not to any extent with the Executive." Unlike Sumner, Stevens, and other Radical Republicans in Congress, the president did not believe that the Southern states had ever left the Union. His proclamation would grant amnesty to the great majority of Southerners who willingly and faithfully subscribed to an oath of future loyalty. Certain classes of Confederates would be excluded from the general amnesty until they applied directly to him and received pardons. These included rebel leaders and those who had mistreated black and white prisoners of war.[15]

Lincoln admitted that "a premature presentation of a plan by the national Executive" on reconstruction "consists in the danger of committals on points which could be more safely left to further developments." He informed Congress that "care has been taken to so shape the document as to avoid embarrassments from this source." "Saying that reconstruction will be accepted if presented in a specific way," he did not mean that "it will never be accepted in any other way." Lincoln also reported that "the movements, by State action, for emancipation," in the border Union states of Missouri and Maryland, "not included in the emancipation proclamation," were "matters of profound gratulation [*sic*]." He concluded, "And while I do not repeat in detail what I have hertofore [*sic*] so earnestly urged" regarding the subjects of Reconstruction and emancipation, "my general views and feelings remain unchanged; and I trust that Congress will omit no fair opportunity of aiding these important steps to a great consummation."[16]

The immediate reaction to the president's reconstruction proclamation and his 1863 annual message, both inside and outside of Congress, was overwhelmingly favorable. In Washington, Lincoln's secretary John Hay recorded in his diary that the effect of the message was "something wonderful. I have never seen such an effect produced by a public document. Men acted as if the Millennium had come." Radical senators Zachariah Chandler and Charles Sumner, Hay noted, expressed delight, "while at the other political pole [James] Dixon & [Reverdy] Johnson said it was highly satisfactory."[17]

In the House of Representatives, Hay wrote, "the effect was the same." Referring to the proclamation, Republican George S. Boutwell of Massachusetts pronounced it "a very able paper. It has great points of popularity: & it is right." Owen Lovejoy of Lincoln's home state and a true abolitionist excitedly told Hay that the document "was glorious," and he now believed that he would live "to see slavery ended in America." Unfortunately, Lovejoy never witnessed the end of slavery; he died in 1864. James A. Garfield, a protégé of Secretary of the Treasury Chase, who opposed the proclamation, defied his political mentor and quietly said, "The President has struck a great blow for the country and himself."[18]

Outside Washington, Horace Greeley's *New York Tribune* and the *Chicago Tribune,* both influential Republican newspapers, praised the reconstruction proclamation for its commitment to emancipation, though they expressed concerns regarding its success in restoring the Union. The editor of the *National Anti-Slavery Standard* predicted that Lincoln "will receive high honors from the lovers of freedom and the haters of slavery everywhere" for his support of emancipation. George Templeton Strong, an antislavery New Yorker who earlier had found little to admire in Lincoln, on December 11 wrote in his later famous diary, "Uncle Abe is the most popular man in America today." The urbane New Yorker predicted, "The firmness, honesty, and sagacity of the 'gorilla despot' may be recognized by the rebels themselves sooner than we expect, and the weight of his personal character may do a great deal toward restoration of our national unity."[19]

Some hard-bitten Republicans in Congress, however, believed that they had a more informed and realistic view of the rebellion than Lincoln. They privately expressed doubts that the president's Proclamation of Amnesty and Reconstruction would have much of an impact on the war and slavery. On December 19, Senator Fessenden wrote to a friend that Lincoln's proclamation was "a silly performance, but he is lucky, & I hope it may work well. Think of telling the rebels they may fight as long as they can, and take a pardon when they have had enough of it."[20] In opposing Lincoln's proclamation, Thaddeus Stevens denied that the president could determine reconstruction policy; only Congress, the Pennsylvania radical insisted, had the authority to formulate a postwar settlement for the South. He characterized Lincoln's Ten Percent Plan as a "mockery of democratic principles." In fact, Stevens declared, the South in rebelling against the Union had reverted to a conquered province status and was subject to Congress's will. Senator Wade said that the plan violated "American principles," and he maintained that "until majorities can be found loyal and trustworthy for state government, [Southerners] must be governed by a stronger hand."[21]

Neither were Democrats and border state conservatives in Congress pleased with the Ten Percent Plan. They simply did not trust Lincoln, believing that he was weak and would succumb to radical pressure on reconstruction. Although most Democrats and virtually all conservatives did not support peace without reunion, they concluded that Lincoln's real purpose in the reconstruction proclamation was to secure Southern electoral votes. Democrats took their cues from the positions of their newspapers and Governor Horatio Seymour of New York in opposing the proclamation. The *New York World*, the bellwether of the northeastern Democratic press, pronounced, "Mr. Lincoln's scheme is not only preposterous in itself, but it is the very height of absurdity to pretend to find authority for it in that part of the Constitution which guarantees to the States a republican form of Government."[22] The *Washington Constitutional Union*, an old Jacksonian Democratic newspaper, declared that the plan would violate a cardinal principle of republicanism—majority rule. This newspaper proposed its own plan for the restoration of the Union: an armistice followed by a national convention of all the states, including the Southern states. The proposal would become the Copperhead platform in 1864, famously advanced by Representative George Pendleton and former congressman Clement Vallandigham, both of Ohio.[23]

In the Senate, Reverdy Johnson of Maryland, having returned to Congress as a conservative leader after an absence of fourteen years, and at first approving of the proclamation, soon joined the Democrats in concluding that the Ten Percent Plan was a scheme to win Republican votes. It would not, he argued, lead to the early return of the rebel states to the Union, as Lincoln said. The Maryland senator declared that the proclamation was a farce and laughed at by the rebels. Johnson, a prominent constitutional lawyer, agreed with Senator Sumner and other Republicans that Congress should determine reconstruction policy. He insisted, however, that the Southern states had never left the Union and should regain all their rights as soon as possible after the surrender of their armies and the replacement of their rebel leaders.[24]

As expected, Confederate spokesmen expressed their contempt for Lincoln's proclamation. The *Richmond Sentinel*, for example, announced that Lincoln's "miserable attempt to divide and conquer us will be contemptuously resented as the insult which it is. . . . This infamous proclamation will arouse us to new zeal and new efforts."[25] The thunderous rebel attacks hurled at the proclamation perhaps inadvertently revealed Confederate concerns that it might have a damaging effect on the Southern war effort.

In Washington, the new Congress essentially adopted a wait-and-see policy toward the president's Ten Percent Plan. In the Senate, it was referred to Lyman Trumbull's Judiciary Committee, where no action was forthcoming. In the House, the Select Committee on the Rebellious States was formed on December 16, 1863, to monitor reconstruction developments under the plan and, if desirable, make recommendations to the full body. The committee was chaired by Henry Winter Davis of Maryland, a political enemy of Lincoln's, who emerged in 1864 as a Radical Republican leader in the House. In the committee, conservative Unionist George H. Yeatman of Kentucky offered a set of resolutions declaring that no formal restoration procedure should be required for the Southern states' return to the Union, and all questions regarding property should be settled by the courts after Southerners reestablished their loyalty. The Republican-dominated committee ignored Yeatman's resolutions.[26]

Republican James M. Ashley, a member of the committee, proposed a bill in the House that, though following the broad outline in Lincoln's plan, would require not only emancipation but also voting rights for black people in the South. The bill, however, disregarded the contention of radicals like Stevens that the rebellious states had also reverted to a territorial or conquered province status. Still, the provision for black suffrage in Ashley's proposal proved too radical for the majority to consider seriously.[27] The House rejected the Ashley bill, and after the Senate Judiciary Committee failed to make a recommendation regarding the president's plan, further deliberations by Congress on reconstruction awaited developments in the war and national politics in 1864.

Meanwhile, the Thirty-Eighth Congress, in coordination with the relevant executive departments, sought to resolve the burgeoning financial problems created by the war. Led by Fessenden in the Senate and Stevens and Elbridge Spaulding in the House, Congress expanded the Civil War income tax rates, adopted other tax measures, and increased the number of Treasury notes in circulation. Although Congress had passed a national banking bill in 1863, it was defective and in need of revision. On June 3, 1864, Congress, with Lincoln's approval, enacted the National Bank Act, which became the basis for the postwar American financial system.[28]

Each bank chartered under the National Bank Act had to purchase a certain number of U.S. bonds, which then could be used as backing for the issuance of "national banknotes." These notes, along with the greenbacks, became a national currency. Many Democratic congressmen and even some Republicans, especially from the West, correctly feared that the national banking system would work to the advantage of northeastern financial interests. The Republican managers of the measure, however, made the compelling case that the creation of a centralized banking system was necessary to aid the war effort by creating monetary stability out of chaos.

In order to further facilitate the construction of the Pacific railway, approved in 1862, Congress in 1864 doubled the amount of aid from $16,000 to $32,000 per mile of completed railroad. The vote was bipartisan and overwhelmingly in favor of the grant; only five senators voted against it. Stevens, chair of the Select Committee on the Pacific Railroad, secured the chartering, along with lavish grants, for a second transcontinental line, which would run from Lake Superior to Puget Sound. Congress also amended the Homestead Act of 1862 and voted to enable Nevada, Colorado, and Nebraska to move toward statehood. In addition, action was taken to encourage immigration from Europe. Lincoln made no objections to any of these measures. Democrats under the leadership of Samuel S. "Sunset" Cox of Ohio in the House and conservative Unionists Reverdy Johnson of Maryland and Lazarus Powell of Kentucky in the Senate attempted at this time to raise the civil liberties issue (for whites) against the administration, but to no avail.[29]

By the spring of 1864, the question of a constitutional amendment ending slavery in America, including the border slave states, had become the focus of congressional deliberations. One week after the new Congress convened in December 1863, Republican James F. Wilson of Iowa introduced in the House the first resolution for an amendment abolishing slavery. Republicans, realizing that they could not obtain the necessary two-thirds majority to pass it, at first hesitated in advancing the resolution for approval. It was ironically a slaveholder, Senator John B. Henderson of Missouri, who gave a boost to the amendment effort when he offered a similar resolution in the Senate Committee of the Whole on January 13, 1864. Henderson saw the handwriting on the wall for slavery's demise; earlier, he had unsuccessfully urged the Missouri legislature to approve Lincoln's gradual, compensated emancipation scheme in order to salvage something from the wreckage of slavery before it was too late. His motion in the Senate was referred to the Judiciary Committee, chaired by Senator Lyman Trumbull, who favored a constitutional amendment to abolish slavery.[30]

On February 15, at the request of Trumbull, Representative Isaac N. Arnold of Illinois offered this resolution in the House: "*Resolved. That the Constitution shall be so amended as to abolish slavery in the United States wherever it now exists, and to prohibit its existence in* every part thereof forever." Democrat William S. Holman of Indiana, who opposed any tampering with slavery, moved to lay Arnold's resolution on the table. Holman's motion failed by a vote of 58 in favor to 79 opposed. Because the vote indicated that supporters of the antislavery amendment still did not have a two-thirds majority for passage (initiation), Wilson by a similar vote had Arnold's resolution referred to the House Committee on the Judiciary for further consideration.[31]

By 1864, President Lincoln clearly wanted a constitutional amendment abolishing slavery. He was especially anxious to have his Emancipation Proclamation validated by an amendment, which would prevent the courts from returning to slavery those black people freed under the proclamation. However, Lincoln remained publicly silent when the amendment was considered. For both constitutional and political reasons, he thought that Congress should take the lead on the issue.[32] Paradoxically, antislavery radicals such as senators Sumner and Wade at first opposed the amendment. They argued for slavery's immediate abolition by congressional legislation in order to avoid the long, drawn-out amending process, which also could fail. On the other hand, Senator John Sherman of Ohio urged the passage of the amendment because he feared that Lincoln's constitutional "conservatism" would cause him to veto an emancipation bill. Trumbull also worried that an act of Congress would not stand the test of constitutionality.[33]

On March 28, 1864, Trumbull from the Judiciary Committee finally introduced Senator Henderson's resolution on the floor of the Senate. He had reworded the resolution to take the form that became the Thirteenth Amendment. Trumbull made a passionate speech in which he emphasized that only a constitutional amendment could ensure that neither a state nor Congress could ever restore slavery.[34] The Illinois senator came under vigorous attack from Senator Morton S. Wilkinson of Minnesota for his refusal to support legislation that would immediately abolish slavery. Senator Henry Wilson, however, in a long speech that he titled "The Death of Slavery Is the Life of the Nation," agreed with Trumbull; he argued that the proposed amendment, not congressional legislation, was necessary to "obliterate the last lingering vestiges of the slave system."[35]

Trumbull, Wilson, and other Republicans also knew that only a constitutional amendment would satisfy conservatives like Republican James Doolittle of Wisconsin and border state Unionists like Reverdy Johnson. Conservative senators had insisted that, as Johnson put it, ending slavery was "not within the scope of either [federal] legislative or executive authority." Indeed, on April 5, the Maryland senator took to the floor of the Senate, announced his support for the amendment, and delivered what prominent journalist Horace White later wrote was "the most impressive speech made in either branch of Congress" on the issue. "The fact that he represented a slaveholding State," White concluded, "[did] not fail to add force to any argument he might make in support of the measure, but the argument itself, both in its moral and its legal aspects, was of surpassing merit. It deserves a high place in the annals of senatorial eloquence." Johnson, who had been a slaveholder in his youth, reminded wavering senators that the institution was "already fatally wounded. If permitted to survive at all, it can survive only to fester and to trouble us." Furthermore, he said, "We have called upon [the freed slaves] to aid us in maintaining the Government" and the Union. "To suffer these men to be reduced to bondage again," Johnson declared, "would be a disgrace to the nation, even greater, if possible, than would be that of reviving the foreign slave trade."[36]

Johnson's speech probably failed to influence any senator to change his vote. However, it must have reinforced in the minds of conservative Republicans Doolittle, Edgar Cowan, and Dixon their support for the amendment; earlier, like Johnson, they had opposed any federal action against slavery. Three days after the Maryland senator's speech, on April 8, the Senate approved the antislavery amendment by a vote of 38 to 6, with 5 senators absent; from the border states, only Senators Johnson and Henderson supported it.[37] The debate and decision on this charter of freedom now moved to the House of Representatives.

There, Republicans needed to persuade at least thirteen Democrats and border state conservatives to vote for the amendment; otherwise, they would not be able to obtain the necessary two-thirds majority for approval. On June 15, Isaac Arnold of Illinois undertook the difficult task of persuasion. In a speech on the floor of the House,

Arnold appealed to "border State men and Democrats of the free States [to] look over your country; see the bloody footsteps of slavery; see the ruin and desolation which it has brought upon our once happy land; and ask, why stay the hand now ready to strike down to death the cause of all these evils?" Arnold warned, "We can have no permanent peace while slavery lives. It now reels and struggles toward its last death-struggle. Let us strike the monster this decisive blow." He exclaimed, "Live a century, nay a thousand years, and no such opportunity to do a great deed for humanity, for liberty, for peace and for your country, will ever again present itself."[38] Ebon C. Ingersoll, also of Illinois, used equally towering words to promise that when the amendment succeeded, "our voices will ascend to Heaven over a country re-united, over a people disenthralled, and God will bless us."[39] Some Radical Republicans, notably Stevens and George W. Julian of Indiana, did not speak, which probably reflected their disappointment that the amendment did not go far enough by guaranteeing equal rights for black people.[40]

Democrats were unmoved by the passionate appeals of Arnold, Ingersoll, and other Republican speakers. Samuel J. Randall of Pennsylvania repeated the Democratic litany of concerns about the amendment. He insisted that the amendment's adoption would open the door to other radical changes in the Constitution and the American system of government. Furthermore, Randall said, the Republican antislavery policy was already uniting the South and dividing the North. The war could not be won if the amendment was approved, he declared. "Gentleman" George Pendleton of Ohio, soon to become the Democratic candidate for vice president, even argued that neither Congress nor three-fourths of the states, which were required to ratify a constitutional amendment, had the power to abolish slavery where it existed. Only one Democrat, Ezra Wheeler of Wisconsin, spoke in favor of the amendment.[41]

The final vote, on June 15, 1864, demonstrated the failure of House Republicans to obtain the votes necessary to initiate the antislavery amendment and send it to the states for ratification: 93 representatives voted in favor and 65 opposed. Twenty-three members, mainly Northern Democrats, including Randall, did not vote.[42] While opposed to the Republican amendment, some members probably failed to vote because they did not want to be on the wrong side of history when slavery ended and, more immediately, on the unpopular side of the issue when seeking reelection.

Infuriated by the rejection of the antislavery amendment by the House of Representatives, Republicans in Congress, as well as elsewhere, determined to make it a campaign issue in the fall election. Horace Greeley's *New York Tribune* immediately announced, "The Democratic party in the House to-day deliberately strapped the burden of Slavery on its shoulders for the coming Presidential election."[43]

Two weeks earlier, on May 31, 1864, a convention consisting mainly of Republican dissidents had met in Cleveland and formed the Radical Democracy Party. They adopted a platform of thirteen planks, including constitutional amendments to abolish slavery and "secure to all men absolute equality before the law." The platform also demanded that Congress, not the president, determine reconstruction policy. In addition, it called for the confiscation of rebel lands and their distribution among "the soldiers and actual [Union?] settlers" in the South.[44] The new party then nominated John C. Frémont, the hero of Missouri radicals, for president. Although Sumner, Wade, Thaddeus Stevens, and a few other radicals in Congress agreed with most of the Cleveland platform, they wisely refused to bolt the Republican Party and support Frémont. Only one radical senator, B. Gratz Brown of Missouri, participated in the Cleveland convention.

One week after the Radical Democracy convention, and one week before the House of Representatives rejected the proposed Thirteenth Amendment, the Republican Party, renamed the National Union Party, met in Baltimore to prepare for the fall election. Aroused to action by the Radical Democracy threat and the antislavery amendment's likely failure in Congress, President Lincoln lobbied for his party's convention to approve a platform supporting the amendment. He specifically asked Senator Edwin D. Morgan of New York to include in his keynote speech to the delegates a statement urging the adoption of the constitutional amendment in the platform. Morgan readily complied. He made a stirring speech in favor of the amendment and also for the uncompromising prosecution of the war to preserve the Union. The delegates adopted the antislavery plank; they probably would have done so whether or not Lincoln, through Morgan, had insisted on it.[45]

Despite the desire of Senator Sumner and other radicals for a commitment to black equality, no mention was made of civil rights in the platform. Such a plank in the platform could have divided the party and severely damaged its chances in the fall elections. Lincoln certainly wanted no such radical declaration by the convention. He must have been pleased that the platform also avoided any statement on whether the president or Congress controlled reconstruction policy, an issue that was becoming increasingly important in Washington. As expected, the Republican, or National Union, convention nominated Lincoln for president, with only 22 dissenting votes, all cast for General U. S. Grant. Still, many Radical Republicans in Congress and elsewhere expressed their opposition, usually privately, to Lincoln's nomination. Representative George W. Julian of Indiana later wrote, "Of the more earnest and thorough-going Republicans in Congress"—he mainly meant radicals—"probably not one in ten favored" Lincoln. Julian, however, exaggerated when he concluded that the president's nomination "was not only very distasteful to a large majority" of Republicans in Congress, "but to many of the most prominent men of the party throughout the country." The Indiana congressman admitted, however, that this feeling "never found its way to the people."[46]

The failure of the military offensives under the overall command of General Grant to defeat the rebel armies, which had begun with great hopes in the spring, had become the main reason for the growing discontent with Lincoln. The war had become a virtual stalemate, characterized by tremendous casualties near Petersburg, Virginia, above Atlanta, and elsewhere in the South.

Republicans who earlier had been ambiguous regarding Lincoln's Proclamation of Amnesty and Reconstruction were now deeply concerned about the president's liberal pardon and amnesty policy. To Julian and many Republicans in Congress, Lincoln's reconstruction, or restoration, plan was naïve, ill timed, and doomed to fail. They believed that it foretold the early return of rebels to power. By late June, even Republicans who were not radicals favored congressional legislation that would ensure a more stringent reconstruction than under the president's plan. They agreed with the radicals that it should include immediate emancipation, in contrast to Lincoln's willingness to accept an apprenticeship arrangement for young black people, and also guarantees for true Unionist control of the restored Southern governments.

With discontent mounting in the North over the armies' lack of progress, determined radicals, their supporters increasing, prepared to openly challenge the president's leadership on reconstruction policy. The partnership between the president and Congress seemed in jeopardy, with the radicals and like-minded Republicans now poised to control reconstruction policy, so it seemed.

The House Select Committee on the Rebellious States, created in December, had come under the control of Maryland congressman Henry Winter Davis, its chairman. Winter Davis, as he was known, had political issues with Lincoln, which boded ill for cooperation between the House of Representatives and the president on reconstruction. Davis especially bristled at Lincoln's tilt toward the congressman's rival in Maryland politics, Postmaster General Montgomery Blair, a conservative. On one occasion, a contentious argument in the White House between the president and Davis led to an infuriated Davis stalking from Lincoln's office. He apparently never returned.[47] On his part, Lincoln had little use for the Maryland congressman. Winter Davis, according to Julian, "had no superior as a writer, debater and orator. . . . His hostility to the President's policy was as sincere as it was intense."[48]

Immediately after Lincoln issued his reconstruction proclamation on December 8, Davis condemned it as "a usurpation" of congressional authority. He specifically objected to the presidential plan for the reorganization of the South before the rebellion had been suppressed. In early 1864, Davis blocked the seating of congressmen chosen by the Lincoln-initiated governments of Louisiana and Arkansas, though representatives of two New Orleans districts had served in the last session of the Thirty-Seventh Congress. On February 15, as chairman of the Select

Committee on the Rebellious States, Davis introduced a congressional plan of reconstruction. At first he seemed willing to compromise with Lincoln on his policy, probably because members of the committee were not yet ready to challenge the president on reconstruction.

The proposed Davis bill retained Lincoln's right to appoint provisional governors and also his 10 percent requirement for Southern elections to civil governments. Unlike the president's plan, the bill provided for ironclad guarantees of loyalty for officials and legislators in the new governments; former Confederates especially would be excluded. The bill, however, rejected the demand of Stevens and a handful of other radicals that the seceded states should be relegated to a territorial status before reconstruction could begin. Although it retained the states as political entities, they would be subject to congressional legislation to ensure "republican forms of government" before readmission to the Union. The Republican majority in Congress thus would determine what constituted republican forms of government in the South. Because of opposition from Democrats, conservative Unionists, and some Republicans, Davis's measure stalled in the House legislative process.[49]

After several weeks of futile off-and-on debate on the reconstruction bill, Winter Davis on May 4, 1864, introduced amendments designed to secure the approval of undecided Republicans. One amendment provided that 50 percent, rather than Lincoln's 10 percent, of the electorate in each state had to subscribe to the ironclad oath of having never supported the rebellion before the president could appoint a provisional governor to begin the process of reconstruction. This meant that the restoration of civil governments would be delayed until after the war. The second amendment excluded from voting state legislators, high public officials, and military officers of colonel or above, leaving rank-and-file rebels, along with Unionists, free to participate in reconstruction. This amendment, Davis argued, softened the provision in the original bill "so that the exclusion merely operate[d] on persons of dangerous political influence."[50]

The Davis amendments satisfied the Republicans' need for Southern loyalty in the early stages of reconstruction but later would not penalize the majority. Both amendments were approved by the House, with many Democrats and conservative Unionists opposing. While Winter Davis had the floor and was defending the bill, Representative Alexander H. Rice of Maine sought to offer an amendment "to strike out the word 'white' wherever it [occurred] in describing the qualifications of voters." Knowing that a debate on black political rights could easily torpedo the bill, Davis sharply informed Rice, "I cannot yield for that or for any other purpose."[51] Also, a radical demand for the confiscation of rebel estates, which the Republican majority realized would have invited a Lincoln veto if approved, was not seriously considered.

In addition to the two amendments, the Davis bill authorized the president to select the provisional governors, who then would have to be confirmed by the Senate, but only after a rebellious state came under military control. Each provisional governor, who would serve until Congress approved the new state government, was directed by the bill to "enroll all white male citizens of the United States resident in the State [and] request each one to take the oath to support the Constitution." If the persons prescribing to the oath were a majority of the persons enrolled, the provisional governor was required to issue a proclamation inviting the "loyal people" to elect delegates to a state convention. To serve in the convention, delegates would have to swear to the ironclad oath. Davis's bill directed that the convention abolish slavery outright and also repudiate the Confederate debt. Other provisions, not inconsistent with the U.S. Constitution, could be included in the new state document. A ratification election would then be held, as well as an election at the same time for officers in the new state government if the voters and Congress approved the state constitution.[52]

On May 4, 1864, the same day that Winter Davis introduced the amended reconstruction bill, the measure passed the House by a partisan vote of 79 in favor and 59 opposed.[53] Entitled a "Bill to guaranty to certain States whose governments have been usurped or overthrown a republican form of government," it then went to the Senate. There, despite the objection of conservative Republican James Doolittle of Wisconsin, it was referred to the Committee on Territories, chaired by Ben Wade. Doolittle had wanted the bill sent to the Judiciary Committee, headed by Lyman Trumbull, who presumably would be less inclined than the radical Wade to press for radical amendments.[54]

Wade proved amendable to the provisions in the Davis bill. The Ohio senator reported the measure to the Senate on May 17, but because of other important matters under consideration during the last days of the session, it was not debated until July 1. Anxious to secure the passage of the reconstruction bill before adjournment on July 4, Wade explained away his own desire for an amendment requiring black (male) political equality in the restored Southern states. "This amendment, if adopted," he told the Senate, "will probably jeopardize the bill; and, as I believe that the provisions of the bill outweigh all such considerations, and at this state of the proceedings that there is no time for discussion upon it." Senator James H. Lane of Kansas, however, wanted the amendment retained, and he called for a vote on it. The amendment failed by a vote of 5 to 24, with 20 senators absent.[55] The reconstruction bill then passed by a vote of 26 to 3. It was sent to the House for consideration of minor amendments, which were approved.

After the House returned the Wade-Davis reconstruction bill to the Senate for a final vote, Senator John S. Carlile of the Restored Government of Virginia launched a rear-guard attack on it. He thundered that the measure was "one of the most revolutionary [actions] that ever was proposed in a deliberative body claiming to represent a free people." The very title of the bill, purporting a right by Congress to legislate a republican form of government in states that constitutionally had never been out of the Union, was revolutionary and "an insult to the understanding of every intelligent man in the nation," Carlile declared. A slaveholder from western Virginia, Carlile insisted that "a republican form of government must emanate and emanate alone from the people that are to be governed. It belongs not to the Congress of the United States," but to the people of the states. He argued that if Congress established the right to impose a government on a state, then it could do so on every subject of legislation, which to Carlile, conservative Unionists, and Democrats was anathema and destructive of states' rights. Wade responded that the rebellion had destroyed republican governments in the South, and Congress had the constitutional authority under the guarantee clause to restore the states under loyal, legitimate governments.[56]

On July 2, the Senate gave its final approval to the Wade-Davis reconstruction bill. It was then sent to the president for his action. Because the bill was not radical in the minds of many Republicans, they hoped that Lincoln would sign it. On July 4, the president went to the Capitol to review and act on the legislation that Congress had passed as the session ended, including the Wade-Davis bill, which, Lincoln complained, had been placed in his hands only one hour earlier. Republican leaders waited anxiously in the congressional halls for Lincoln's decision on the reconstruction measure. Having heard nothing, Senator Zachariah Chandler of Michigan entered the president's room and asked him if he had signed the bill. "No," Lincoln replied, and indicated that he did not plan to do so, which meant a pocket veto of it. Chandler, a leading radical, told him that "it would make a terrible record for us to fight if it were vetoed." The president answered, "Mr. Chandler, this bill was placed before me a few minutes before Congress adjourned. It is too much to be swallowed in that way."[57] Lincoln was a bit disingenuous, since he probably did not plan to sign it anyway.

Chandler further argued that a veto of the bill "will damage us fearfully in the North West. It may not in Illinois; it will in Michigan and Ohio. The important point is that one prohibiting slavery in the reconstructed States." Lincoln quickly responded, "That is the point on which I doubt the authority of Congress to act." Still, Chandler did not give up. He reminded the president, "It is no more than you have done yourself" in issuing the Emancipation Proclamation. However, Lincoln pointed out that "in an emergency," which the Union faced during the war, the president could "do things on military grounds that cannot be done constitutionally by Congress." With this, the Michigan senator said, "Mr. President I cannot controvert yr. position by argument. I can only say I deeply regret it."[58]

After Chandler left, Senator Fessenden entered the room, and Lincoln explained to him that he could "not see how any of us now can deny and contradict all we have always said, that congress has no constitutional power over slavery in the States." Fessenden agreed and admitted, "I even had my doubts as to the constitutional efficacy of your own decree of emancipation, in such cases where it has not been carried into effect by the actual advance of the army." Lincoln added that supporters of the Wade-Davis bill, in asserting that the rebel states were no longer in the Union, "make the fatal admission . . . that states whenever they please may of their own motion dissolve their connection with the Union," a conclusion, the president told Fessenden, he had "laboriously endeavored to avoid. . . . It was to obviate this question that I earnestly favored the movement for an amendment to the Constitution abolishing slavery." Lincoln said that whether the Southern states had been "in or out of the Union during the war [was] a merely metaphysical question and one unnecessary to be forced into discussion." John Hay, a Lincoln secretary, reported that Secretary of State Seward and Secretary of the Interior John P. Usher, who were also in the room, "seemed entirely in accord with this" view.[59]

After leaving the Capitol, John Hay remarked to the president that, though Zachariah Chandler was popular, he did not think that the senator had accurately reflected public opinion in the meeting. Hay indicated to Lincoln that he did not believe the Radical Republicans "would bolt their ticket" in the presidential election "on a question of metaphysics." He meant a party schism over reconstruction if Lincoln vetoed the Wade-Davis bill. Lincoln made this revealing comment to Hay: "If they choose to make a point upon this I do not doubt that they can do harm. They have never been friendly to me & I dont [sic] know that this will make any special difference as to that. At all events, I must keep some consciousness of being somewhere near right: I must keep some standard of principle fixed within myself."[60]

On July 8, Lincoln issued a proclamation explaining his pocket veto of the Wade-Davis reconstruction bill. In addition to a more formal statement of the reasons he gave Senator Chandler for refusing to sign the measure, the president saw the need to placate the middle-of-the-road Republicans who had supported the bill. He announced that he was "fully satisfied with the system for restoration contained in the Bill, as one very proper plan for the loyal people of any State choosing to adopt it." Indeed, Lincoln promised to assist people in the former rebel states desiring to be reconstructed under the congressional plan.[61] However, he must have known that Southern Union leaders who had attached themselves to his policy would not want to support the complicated and stringent congressional method of reconstruction. In addition, it would have been remarkable if any state chose to implement the congressional reconstruction plan, since the Wade-Davis bill had no legal basis without the president's signature.

Winter Davis, who had remained at his desk as the session ended, rose from his seat when he heard of the pocket veto of his bill. "Pale with wrath, his bushy hair tousled, and wildly brandishing his arms, he denounced the President in good set terms," according to a report.[62] Lincoln's proclamation giving Southern states an option for implementing reconstruction did nothing to placate the bill's Republican supporters. Representative James G. Blaine of Maine later wrote that if Congress had remained in session, the president would have faced "a very rancorous hostility" from members of his party because of the veto.[63]

As it was, some outraged Republicans such as Thaddeus Stevens saw a political motive in the president's veto and subsequent proclamation. "What an infamous proclamation!" Stevens wrote to the Republican clerk of the House of Representatives. "The Pres. Is determined to have the electoral votes of the seceded States," Stevens charged. "The idea of pocketing a bill and then issuing a proclamation as to how far he would conform to it, is matched only by signing a bill and then sending in a veto. How little of the rights of war and the law of nations our Pres. knows! But what are we to do? Condemn privately and applaud publicly?"[64] The Pennsylvania radical hoped that the Republican Party would reconvene its national convention and choose another candidate for president, perhaps General Benjamin F. Butler.

Although Stevens and most Republicans shied away from publicly attacking the president, Ben Wade and Winter Davis had no such qualms. The fact that the war continued to go badly for the Union during the summer contributed to their determination to censure the president for his veto. When Lincoln issued his July 8 proclamation explaining his veto of the Wade-Davis bill, a Confederate force commanded by General Jubal Early had entered Maryland and was marching toward Washington, only to be stopped on the outskirts of the city. Elsewhere, Grant's and Sherman's armies were bogged down in the South and suffering tremendous casualties. The grim military and political events of the fall and winter of 1862–63 seemed to be repeating themselves in 1864, and Wade and Davis wanted to take advantage of the growing discontent of the Union people with Lincoln.

Nonetheless, their outrage seemed genuine. Wade and Davis issued a blistering public criticism of the president's veto. Printed in the *New York Tribune* on August 5, the Wade-Davis Manifesto, as it became known, declared of Lincoln's veto, "A more studied outrage on the legislative authority of the people has never [before] been perpetrated." The lengthy manifesto derided the "shadow governments" that the president had created in Louisiana and Arkansas. They were "mere creatures of his will . . . imposed on the people by military orders under the form of election, at which generals, provost marshals, soldiers, and camp-followers were the chief actors, assisted by a handful of resident citizens, and urged on to premature action by private letters from the President."[65]

Wade and Davis scornfully predicted that before the fall presidential election, governments similar to the one in Louisiana would be "organized in every rebel State where the United States has a camp." The president "must understand," they declared, "that our support is of a cause and not of a man; that the authority of Congress is paramount and must be respected." Wade and Davis called on the supporters of the government in Congress, when they met in December, to resist the "usurpations" of power by Lincoln; if they did not, they would be "justly liable to the indignation of the people whose rights and security, committed to their keeping, they sacrifice."[66]

If Wade and Davis expected support for their manifesto from other Republican congressmen, they would be sadly disappointed. Although many Republican members opposed the president's veto, the harsh and obviously personal attack of the protest caused them to ignore or repudiate it. Occurring at a time when support for the war and the political fortunes of the party had dipped to a low point, Republicans in Congress could not politically—or for the sake of the Union—afford to endorse the manifesto. The Copperheads had taken over the national Democratic Party, which would meet in late August in Chicago to adopt a platform and nominate a candidate for president. Republican congressman James G. Blaine later wrote that the "great majority of the loyal people" realized that "the pending struggle for the Presidency demanded harmony," and they made clear to their representatives in Congress that the Wade-Davis Manifesto would have only created "dissension and division" in Unionist ranks.[67]

Influential Republican newspapers also refused to support the Wade-Davis Manifesto. The *Chicago Tribune* deplored the action of Wade and Davis, commenting, "Those who love the Union cause owe them no thanks for their hot-heated precipitancy." Even Greeley's *New York Tribune*, which had printed the manifesto, backed off from endorsing it. Henry J. Raymond, the new chairman of the Republican National Committee and editor of the *New York Times*, declared that in Wade's and Davis's eyes, "the real crime of President Lincoln . . . is not that he has in any way or to any extent invaded the rights of Congress, or usurped power . . . but he has evinced a purpose to restore the states to their old allegiance, and the Union to its old integrity, upon terms more in conformity with the spirit of Republican Government than those which they seek to impose."[68]

Lincoln pretended to ignore the Wade-Davis Manifesto, though he was clearly angered by it. When Secretary of the Navy Welles mentioned to Lincoln that he had seen the protest of Wade and Davis, the president dismissed it and remarked, "Well, let them wriggle." On another occasion, Lincoln commented that from what had been reported about the manifesto, he had no desire to read it. He indicated that he would not take part "in such a controversy as they seemed to wish to provoke." The ever-suspicious Welles believed that Davis, who had drawn Wade and others into his scheme, was seeking to replace Lincoln as the Republican candidate for president.[69] Indeed, Davis had become part of a group, including prominent Republicans of New York City, that met in mid-August to draft plans to hold another national convention to supplant Lincoln as the party's nominee.[70] But in September, the war and the political situation in the North turned dramatically in favor of Lincoln and the Republicans, and the convention movement collapsed.

TRIUMPH AND TRAGEDY

As soon became clear, the Democratic National Convention, meeting in Chicago in late August, provided Lincoln and the Republicans with the political gift they needed. It adopted the Copperhead platform, pronouncing the war a failure and calling for a cease-fire to be followed by a national convention to restore the Union. The convention also demanded the restoration of the rights of the states as they had existed before the war, which suggested the continuation of slavery if the Democrats won the election. With good reason, Lincoln and the Republicans, as well as many disturbed Democrats and conservative Unionists, believed that the Democratic platform was a recipe for Confederate independence. The Democrats at Chicago did little to ease this concern when, on August 31, they nominated McClellan, an ill-starred general, for president and Copperhead congressman George Pendleton for vice president.

Two days later, the telegraph wires flashed the news that General Sherman had taken Atlanta, preceded by Admiral David Farragut's capture of Mobile Bay. Morale in the Union states revived, but no one could be sure what might happen on the battlefield before the November election. Sobered by the Democratic peace platform, radicals as well as other Republicans closed ranks behind the president. Their support for Lincoln was made easier by the forced resignation of Postmaster General Montgomery Blair, who, along with Seward, had become the bête noire of the radicals in the cabinet. Senator Zachariah Chandler played an important role in engineering the removal of Blair, simultaneously with the withdrawal of John C. Frémont as the candidate of the Radical Democracy Party.[1] This third party of disgruntled radicals and abolitionists, though weakened since its establishment in May, might have siphoned off critical votes from the Republicans if Frémont had remained a candidate.

In September, Chandler, Wade, Stevens, and other radical congressmen, fearful of a Democratic victory, reluctantly fell in line and campaigned for the Lincoln–Andrew Johnson ticket. Wade wrote to Chandler, "Were it not for the country there would be poetic justice in [Lincoln] being beaten by that stupid ass McClellan. . . . I can but wish the d——l had Old Abe. But the issue is now made up and we have to take him, or Jeff Davis, for McClellan and all who will support him, are meaner traitors than are to be found in the Confederacy."[2] While supporting Lincoln in the fall campaign, radicals and other Republican congressmen emphasized the disastrous consequences of a Copperhead victory in the election. "Elect McClellan," Stevens told a rally in Pennsylvania, "and our Republic has ceased to exist. Reelect the calm statesman who now presides over the nation, and he will lead you to an honorable peace and to permanent liberty."[3] The fact that Lincoln during the dark days of August had stood firmly behind the party's antislavery and Union platform also must have had some influence on Stevens and other Republican leaders in their willingness to campaign for him.

The impressive success of Lincoln and the Republicans in the fall 1864 elections and the realization that the rebellion was on its last legs strengthened the president's position in the nation as well as that of his party in Congress. Representative George W. Julian, a radical and member of the War Committee who had found Lincoln greatly deficient in the necessary qualities of leadership, admitted that since the election, his Republican colleagues "don't want any quarrel with Lincoln." Julian concluded, "Old Abe, through his patronage, is the virtual dictator of the country."[4]

Although Julian exaggerated Lincoln's power, "Old Abe" no doubt had become master of affairs in Washington. Nonetheless, as the war entered its final phase and there seemed no longer a need for a united front, Republicans in Congress more openly than before challenged the president's policies, particularly on reconstruction. Despite an increase in Republican members as a result of the fall elections, the new Congress could not be sworn in until March 4, 1865, or later, provided the president decided to call a special session. The last session of the old Congress, which convened on December 5, 1864, would end on March 3. On one thing the Republicans in Congress and Lincoln could readily agree: the elections had willed the adoption of the amendment abolishing slavery. Although Republican leaders in the old House of Representatives did not have the necessary two-thirds majority to reverse the amendment's rejection in June, they hoped that enough Democrats and conservative Unionists could be persuaded to support it before the end of the session.

One day after Congress assembled, Lincoln submitted his annual message, which, as it turned out, was his last one. As expected, the president recommended the reconsideration and passage of the proposed Thirteenth Amendment by the House of Representatives. He explained that "the abstract question" regarding the amendment had "not changed; but an intervening election shows, almost certainly that the next Congress will pass the measure if this [one] does not. Hence there is only a question of *time* as to when the proposed amendment will go to the States for their action. . . . May we not agree that the sooner the better?" Lincoln declared, "It is the voice of the people now, for the first time, heard upon the question," and Congress should pay "deference . . . to the will of the majority, simply because it is the will of the majority. In this case the common end is the maintenance of the Union," Lincoln said. And the abolition of slavery was "among the means to secure that end."[5]

On the question of peace, the president stated that "no attempt at negotiation with the insurgent leader could result in any good. He would accept nothing short of severance of the Union—precisely what we will not and cannot give. . . . It is an issue which can only be tried by war; and decided by victory."[6] This was music to the ears of many Republicans in Congress, who feared that once he had won the election, Lincoln would be agreeable to a negotiated peace with the rebel leaders, perhaps abandoning immediate emancipation to secure reunion.

Lincoln devoted more than four pages to a report on foreign affairs, in which he glossed over America's strained relations with Great Britain. He barely mentioned the "unforeseen political difficulties" that had arisen with Britain over neutral rights at sea and in ports and the "recent assaults and depredations committed by inimical and desperate persons" operating from Canadian bases. However, he believed that Canadian authorities, with the approval of the British government, would "take the necessary measures to prevent new incursions across the border."[7] Without referring to the French in Mexico, the president wrote that "Mexico continues to be a theatre of civil war," a conflict in which America maintained a strict neutrality.[8]

The president reported favorably on the national banking system, created by Congress in 1863; he insisted that it had been accepted by the "capitalists" and the public. His financial account was a summary of the report of Secretary of the Treasury William Pitt Fessenden, who had replaced Salmon P. Chase after his removal in June 1864. Fessenden at first rejected the appointment, only to accept it after Lincoln told him that he "had no right to decline," since "Providence" had pointed him out for the position.[9] The appointment proved a wise choice. As chairman of the Senate Finance Committee, the New Englander had had a leading role, along with Chase, in shaping the financial policies of the government, including the National Bank Act. A quick-tempered New Englander who did not always appreciate Lincoln's quips and anecdotes, Fessenden came to support the president and oppose radical legislation.

Lincoln reported that "changes from State systems to the national system [were] rapidly taking place." Soon, he believed, there would be "no banks of issue not authorized by Congress, and no bank-note circulation not secured by the government." The old Whig views of both Lincoln and Fessenden were clearly evident in the president's prediction that "the government and the people will derive great benefit from the change in the banking systems of the country." Lincoln promised that the new system "will create a reliable and permanent influence in support of the national credit, and protect the people against losses in the use of paper money."[10] Neither Lincoln nor Fessenden, however, could foresee the future when financial assets under the National Bank Act, as amended, would be controlled by northeastern financial interests to the detriment of the American people and banking elsewhere.

The president in his 1864 annual message also summarized the secretary of the interior's report on western affairs. The president announced that the "great enterprise of connecting the Atlantic with the Pacific States by railways and telegraph lines has been entered upon with a vigor that gives assurance of success." He reminded Congress of his recommendation in his "last message that our Indian system be remodeled." These reforms, Lincoln wrote, should provide for "the welfare of the Indian" and also protect "the advancing settler."[11] The report of the November 29, 1864, massacre of approximately 130 Cheyenne and Arapaho Indians at Sand Creek by Colorado territorial troops under the command of Colonel John M. Chivington came too late for the president to mention it in his annual message.

Soon, however, news of the Sand Creek massacre reached Washington, stunning members of Congress. Senator James Doolittle, chairman of the Committee on Indian Affairs and a Lincoln ally, declared that the report of the vicious attack should "make one's blood almost chill and freeze with horror."[12] Likewise, Senator Charles Sumner pronounced the massacre "an exceptional crime; one of the most atrocious in the history of any country." Republican senator James Harlan of Iowa expressed concern that a military operation was planned against the Comanches by General James H. Carleton, a known Indian fighter, which could provoke a general war in the West. Harlan gravely predicted that if war occurred, "we shall have to suffer the disgrace of the extermination of thousands of these comparatively inoffensive and unarmed people."[13]

The Doolittle committee launched an investigation into the Sand Creek massacre. It condemned Colonel Chivington, but he never faced disciplinary action. The committee, which produced its final report in 1867, blamed the violence in the West on "the aggressions of lawless white men" and the loss of tribal hunting grounds to miners, railroads, and settlers. Doolittle, who wrote the report, doubted, however, that anything could be done to prevent the conflict in the West until "the Indian race is civilized or shall entirely disappear," a

rather disturbing conclusion for someone who professed to sympathize with the western Indians. The committee did make one important recommendation. It urged Congress to create a Board of Indian
Commissioners, which was realized four years after the committee's
report. With mixed results, the board functioned until 1934.[14]

Lincoln ended his 1864 annual message with a strong statement on
how peace could be achieved in the Civil War. In it, he also reaffirmed
his commitment to black freedom as set forth in the Emancipation
Proclamation and the acts of Congress. He announced, "In stating
a simple condition of peace, I mean simply to say that the war will
cease on the part of the government, whenever it shall cease on the
part of those who began it." At the same time, Lincoln declared
that he would "retract nothing" he had said in the Emancipation
Proclamation, nor would he return to slavery any person freed by
the proclamation or by Congress. "If the people should, by whatever
mode or means, make it an Executive duty to re-enslave such persons,
another, and not I, must be their instrument to perform it."[15]

The president's message was well received by Republicans in Congress; even Stevens approved it. Stevens praised the message for its
brevity and treatment of "subjects of great importance, not only to
this nation, but to the whole family of man." He specifically meant
Lincoln's call for the passage of the abolition amendment. "I do not
think I am extravagant when I say it is the most important and best
message that has been communicated to Congress for the last 60
years. . . . Although the President never made much pretension to
a polished education," Stevens could not find "the least fault" with
the composition of the message. He concluded that there never was a
time when the president stood so high in the opinion of the people—
and Congress.[16] Despite his praise for the message, the Pennsylvania
radical did not withhold his criticism of Lincoln, particularly the
president's refusal to support a stringent reconstruction policy and
equal rights for black people in the South.

Not all members of Congress approved of Lincoln's annual message. As expected, the Democrats found fault with it. James Brooks
of New York, a spokesman for the dwindling ranks of Copperheads

in Congress, took to the floor of the House on December 14 and offered two objections to the message, followed by an hour-and-a-half speech laced with historical references to slavery in support of his position. He was frequently interrupted by Republican members who challenged his facts of history. As if the fall election had not occurred, Brooks vigorously objected to the president's contention, "first, that the war must go on without further negotiations; and, second, that the war must go on until the abolition of slavery is made perpetual throughout all portions of the old United States." He repeated the Copperhead mantra that the war could not be won by bayonets alone, especially if Lincoln and the Republicans insisted on emancipation as a condition for peace.[17] Along with like-minded Democratic colleagues, Brooks soon attempted to block approval by the House of the Thirteenth Amendment.

At least one Republican, Henry Winter Davis, chairman of the House Committee on Foreign Affairs, attacked the president's failure in his annual message to denounce the French intervention in Mexico and announce that America would not tolerate it. Earlier, on April 4, 1864, Davis had secured unanimous approval by the House of a resolution that members of Congress were "unwilling by silence, to leave the nations of the world under the impression that they [were] indifferent spectators of the deplorable events now transpiring in the Republic of Mexico." In addition, Winter Davis wanted the House of Representatives to issue his committee's report on the French refusal to abandon their imperial ambitions in Mexico. He had become upset when he learned of a letter from Secretary of State Seward reassuring the French foreign minister that Congress had no role in the matter. With other issues pending and the war at a critical stage during the spring of 1864, the House did not release the Davis committee report.[18]

Winter Davis, however, refused to concede defeat. On December 15, after reading Lincoln's annual message, Davis defiantly introduced a resolution in the House maintaining "that Congress [had] a constitutional right to an authoritative voice in declaring and prescribing the foreign policy of the United States." The resolution declared that it was "the constitutional duty of the President to respect that policy."

Republican John Farnsworth of Illinois immediately moved to table the Davis resolution, whereupon "Sunset" Cox of Ohio called for a roll-call vote on the tabling question. Like Davis, Cox, a leading Democrat and a member of the Committee on Foreign Affairs, was also disturbed by Seward's letter in which he virtually apologized to the French for the House's attempt to have a hand in foreign policy. Without debate, Farnsworth's motion to table passed by a vote of 69 to 63, with 50 representatives not voting. The vote was largely along party lines, but with Radical Republicans Thaddeus Stevens and James M. Ashley of Ohio joining Davis on the losing side.[19] Stevens and Ashley, like Davis, wanted the House to have an authoritative role in foreign affairs.

Winter Davis and Cox immediately resigned from the Committee on Foreign Affairs. In resigning, Davis issued a blistering attack on the president for ignoring the will of Congress as expressed in the House resolution of April 4, 1864, regarding French imperialism in Mexico. The members of the committee, Davis said, regretted that "the President should have thought proper to inform a foreign government of a radical and serious conflict of opinion and jurisdiction between . . . the legislative and executive power of the United States." They also "learned with surprise" that the president had concluded that "a monarchical government imposed on a neighboring republic [was] a 'purely executive question.'" Davis announced, with questionable historical accuracy, that "no President has ever claimed such an exclusive authority." He insisted that Congress should not permit Lincoln's assertion of complete executive control "to pass without dissent." Remarkably, the Maryland congressman maintained, "There is no word in that resolution which assails the President, nor was it contemplated to assail him," a denial that must have amused House members who knew otherwise.[20]

Davis succeeded in shaming House members into reconsidering his resolution. Regardless of their position on the resolution, Republicans did not want to lose the powerful voice of Winter Davis in the House by repudiating him while congressional debate over important issues such as the Thirteenth Amendment and reconstruction was pending. Many Democrats favored the Davis resolution as a way to embarrass the Lincoln administration. In the debate on the resolution, its Republican supporters aimed their fire at Seward rather than Lincoln, whom they did not want to antagonize. Secretary of the Navy Welles recorded in his diary, "[Davis], Thad Stevens, and others had an opportunity to ventilate their feelings. They do not like Seward and are runing [*sic*] their heads and putting their hands into all sorts of mischief and indiscretion to relieve their hostility."[21]

Supporters of the Davis resolution won the day in the House of Representatives. The resolution claiming congressional authority in foreign relations passed the House by a vote of 68 to 59. Conservative Unionists and all but two Democrats joined 16 Republicans in voting for the resolution. A few Republicans, who probably favored the resolution but did not want to antagonize Lincoln, deliberately absented themselves from the vote.[22]

In the upper chamber, Republican senators took their cue from Charles Sumner, chairman of the Foreign Affairs Committee, who opposed the Davis resolution. Despite their dislike of Seward and the administration's appeasement policy toward the French, the senators sensed public opposition to the resolution and refused to challenge the president on the issue. The Republican press also denounced the resolution.[23] For example, the *New York Times*, whose editor Henry Raymond was chairman of the Republican National Committee, condemned the House resolution as "little more than a splenetic ebullition against the President, on the part of those who failed to prevent his re-election." When the Senate declined to consider the House resolution, the controversy over control of foreign affairs subsided.[24]

President Lincoln and Republicans in Congress were in complete agreement on one issue during the winter session of 1864–65. This was the fulfillment of the party's platform for the approval of the Thirteenth Amendment abolishing slavery. The story of the House of Representatives' action on the amendment resolution in January 1865 is a familiar one, made popular by the movie *Lincoln*. Although the Senate had approved the resolution in June, the amendment had failed to secure the necessary two-thirds for passage in the House, with almost all Northern Democrats and border state conservatives voting against it. Lincoln had reminded Congress in his annual message that in the November election, "the voice of the people now, for the first time," had spoken for the amendment's approval, and the people demanded immediate adoption of it.

Both Lincoln and Representative James M. Ashley, who sponsored the resolution in the House, hoped that in view of the election results, at least twelve Democrats and conservatives would change their votes and provide the margin of victory for the amendment. In introducing the amendment resolution on January 6, Ashley quoted the president's famous Hodges letter of April, 4, 1864, "If slavery is not wrong, nothing is wrong." Ashley told House members that because "slavery is wrong and criminal, as the great body of enlightened and Christian men [also] admit, it is certainly our duty to abolish it."[25] Lincoln and Ashley, however, realized that it would require a major effort on their part to persuade reluctant members to vote for it. The Ohio congressman particularly saw the need to reassure skeptical conservatives in his party that the enforcement section in the amendment, which some of his radical colleagues wanted, was designed to guarantee only emancipation and not suffrage or other civil rights. Still, when the debate began in January 1865 on the amendment resolution, Ashley was fearful that the necessary two-thirds majority for approval could not be obtained. Democrats and conservative border state representatives, as before, seemed solidly opposed to the amendment.

At this juncture, the president launched an intensive and, for him, rare lobbying campaign to secure the critical votes for the resolution in the House of Representatives. He wanted the amendment initiated by Congress and sent to the states for ratification before the Thirty-Eighth Congress adjourned sine die on March 3. It was likely, however, that if the House failed to support the amendment, Lincoln would call a special session of the new Congress in the spring, in which the Republicans would have a two-thirds majority and would immediately approved it. But Lincoln wanted the old Congress to act soon after the election and before unforeseen complications developed.

Lincoln focused his lobbying efforts on middle-of-the-road Democratic opponents such as "Sunset" Cox, who claimed to be his friend, and also border state Unionists who in June had voted against the amendment. Although he had led the president to believe that he would support the amendment, "Sunny," as Lincoln called Cox, voted against it. In the end, only a handful of Northern Democrats switched their votes. The president had better success with border state conservatives. Early in January, he called Representative James S. Rollins of Missouri to the White House to seek his support. Rollins, a slaveholder, later recalled that Lincoln began by reminding him, "You and I were old whigs, both of us followers of the great statesman, Henry Clay, and I tell you I never had an opinion upon the subject of slavery in my life that I did not get from him." If enough border state members united to pass the amendment, Lincoln told Rollins, the rebels "would soon see that they could not expect much help from that quarter"; they then would "quit their war upon the government."[26]

The president had made the same argument to the border state congressmen in 1862, only to be rebuffed. But by early 1865, the situation had changed, and the border states themselves were adopting emancipation ordinances. Not only did Rollins indicate that he would vote for the amendment, but he also promised to speak in favor of it and persuade other border state members to support it. True to his word, the Missourian gave a long antislavery speech in the House on January 13; he also succeeded in obtaining the backing of other conservative colleagues.[27]

By late January, it appeared that Lincoln, Ashley, and supporters of the Thirteenth Amendment had enough votes to carry the amendment, though by only a razor-thin margin. But a major complication arose, which was partly of the president's own making. On December 28, Francis P. Blair Sr., patriarch of a politically prominent family of Maryland, asked for and received a pass from Lincoln to visit Richmond and talk to Jefferson Davis, ostensibly to recover personal papers seized in the July Confederate raid on Maryland by General Jubal Early's forces. Blair's main purpose, however, was as an unofficial envoy to initiate peace negotiations. On January 12, Blair met with Davis, who had once stayed in his Maryland home. The Confederate president agreed to negotiate with the Lincoln government, but only "with a view to secure peace to the *two countries*."[28]

Lincoln, of course, could not agree to peace on the basis of the "two countries." However, three Confederate commissioners, including Vice President Alexander H. Stephens, soon appeared at General Grant's headquarters in City Point, Virginia, and asked, without mentioning the "two countries" conundrum, for permission to meet with Lincoln. On the morning of the scheduled House vote on the antislavery amendment, January 31, a report circulated that rebel peace negotiators had entered Union lines and were en route to Washington. The report caused proamendment Democrats and conservatives in the House to waver in their support of the resolution, believing that peace with reunion might soon be achieved if emancipation was not made a condition for negotiations. Ashley frantically sent Lincoln a note asking the president to deny the report that the rebel commissioners were on their way to Washington; otherwise, "if it is true," Ashley told him, "I fear that we shall lose the bill [resolution]." Although earlier in the day, Lincoln had decided to send Secretary of State Seward to Fort Monroe in Virginia for a possible meeting with the Confederate commissioners, he gave Ashley the answer that he needed. "So far as I know," he wrote disingenuously, "there are no peace commissioners in the city, or likely to be in it."[29]

The president's reassurance to Ashley had the desired effect. The vote in the House on the Thirteenth Amendment was 119 in favor to 56 opposed, barely attaining the necessary two-thirds majority for approval, and Lincoln then sent the historic document to the states for ratification. Two days after the House of Representatives approved the Thirteenth Amendment, General Grant, who still detained the Confederate peace commissioners, telegraphed the president advising that it would be a mistake not to see them. The commissioners, he said, had good intentions and a desire "to restore peace and union." Hoping that something could come of it, Lincoln immediately went to Hampton Roads, Virginia, to join Seward in a conference with the Confederates. Nothing, however, came of the meeting, though Lincoln unrealistically proposed a compensation plan for Southern slave losses to facilitate a rebel capitulation and emancipation.[30]

When radicals Stevens, Chandler, Sumner, and Wade heard of the Blair mission to Richmond and later also learned that Lincoln would meet with the Confederate commissioners, they were furious. Senator Chandler, who blamed the affair on Seward, expressed the radicals' view when he wrote soon after the peace failure: "The whole proceedings was not only disgraceful but ridiculous. . . . I hope we shall have no more meetings of fools untill [sic] the Rebellion is ended & then that wise men will take their places."[31] Chandler and the radicals had feared that Lincoln would agree to a cease-fire followed by a compromise peace with the rebels and the surrender of immediate emancipation.[32] Radicals as well as other Republicans, and even many Democrats and border state conservatives, were relieved when they learned that the president at Hampton Roads had stood firm behind the Union war aims.

Nonetheless, Congress asked but did not demand that Lincoln provide a report on the Blair mission and the Hampton Roads conference. The president agreed after Speaker of the House Schuyler Colfax assured him that his report on the negotiations and their results "cannot fail to increase the confidence of the American people in you."[33] When the Senate considered asking for the report, James Doolittle, a Republican friend of the president, engaged in a bitter exchange with Ben Wade. The Wisconsin senator charged that a radical and Democratic plot sought to undermine the authority of the president. He asserted that Wade had always been antagonistic to Lincoln. Wade leaped to the floor, denounced Doolittle, and, incredibly, announced, "I have not criticized the president at all." He denied that despite his many differences with Lincoln, he was hostile to him.[34]

On February 10, Lincoln submitted his report to Congress on the events associated with the peace negotiations. When the clerk in the House of Representatives completed the reading of the report, including documents, "an instant and irrepressible storm of applause" erupted, according to an observer.[35] Stevens admitted that the radicals had been wrong about Lincoln's peace effort. "I do not believe there was a man on this side who desired to sue for peace. But the President thought it was best to make the effort, and he has done it in such a masterly style, upon such a firm basis and principle, that I believe [all] who thought his mission there was unwise will accord to him sagacity and patriotism, and applaud his action."[36] Even Fernando Wood, New York's most notorious Copperhead, praised Lincoln's firmness in preserving "the integrity of the American Union" at Hampton Roads.[37]

With the Union victory in sight in early 1865, the issue of reconstruction, in addition to the ending of slavery, had assumed major importance; it would test the postelection harmony between the president and Congress. On December 15, 1864, Representative Ashley of the House Select Committee on the Rebellious States put forth a bill "to guarantee to certain States whose governments have been usurped or overthrown a republican form of government." The proposed bill, while similar in some respects to the Wade-Davis bill, which Lincoln had pocket vetoed, was designed by the committee to satisfy the president. Although it generally retained the Wade-Davis procedure in the reconstruction process, the Ashley bill maintained the president's authority in the appointment of provisional governors and the reorganization of loyal governments. As a further concession to Lincoln, the bill recognized his government in Louisiana without any significant change. (Arkansas was later added.) Ashley and the committee members also believed that the proposed bill would secure the approval of the majority in Congress, as it avoided radical provisions, measures that conservative Republicans, Democrats, and border state Unionists, especially in the Senate, would oppose.[38]

The Ashley bill required immediate emancipation, but like the earlier Wade-Davis bill, it limited the voters in the reconstruction elections to "loyal male citizens," which conservatives viewed as a circuitous route to enfranchise black male adults. Even Lincoln at first seemed to think that this would be the case. Whereas Lincoln's Ten Percent Plan included a liberal loyalty oath, the Ashley bill specified that only those loyal citizens who could take the ironclad oath swearing that they had never aided the rebellion would be eligible to participate in the first elections or serve as jurors.

In essence, the Ashley bill proposed a joint role for the president and Congress in reconstruction. The question was, would the president agree to abandon his Ten Percent Plan for the nine Southern states covered by the Ashley bill? Historians have contended that

Lincoln was willing to endorse the measure to obtain congressional approval of his Louisiana and Arkansas governments. Their conclusion rests mainly on marginal notations that he made on a printed copy of the bill. But a close reading of the holograph document in the Lincoln Papers reveals that the notations were only for a quick reference to the Ashley measure's provisions, not indicators of his support for the bill.[39]

Nonetheless, Lincoln wanted to avoid a fight with his party in Congress over the Ashley bill. As was his tendency in considering controversial legislation, he sought to find positive features in the Ashley measure while expressing his reservations. In a meeting with General Nathaniel Banks, who had been reappointed to military command in Louisiana, and Montgomery Blair, Lincoln, according to John Hay, commented that he "had been reading [the bill] carefully & said that he liked it with the exception of one or two things which he thought rather calculated to conceal a feature which might be objectionable to some. The first was that . . . negroes would be made jurors & voters under the temporary governments." General Banks, who, like Lincoln, favored limited black suffrage by state action, not by Congress, replied, "What you refer to would be a fatal objection to the Bill. It would simply throw the [state] Government into the hands of the blacks, as the white people under that arrangement would refuse to vote." Banks, who wanted the Louisiana Union government approved by Congress, assured Lincoln that the qualifications for voting and jury duty in the Ashley bill would be restricted to white male citizens.[40]

Lincoln's second reservation concerned the bill's "declaration that all persons heretofore held in slavery are declared free," which he believed was ambiguous. It seemed to the lawyerly president "to be not a prohibition of slavery by Congress but a mere assurance of freedom to persons actually then [free] in accordance with the proclamation of Emancipation."[41] Pending the approval of the Thirteenth Amendment, Lincoln wanted explicit congressional approval of his antislavery actions; otherwise, the courts might find them unconstitutional.

To satisfy the president and conservative congressmen, Ashley altered the bill by striking out the provisions designed to permit black voting and jury service. Ashley's radical colleagues were furious with him. Winter Davis, Thaddeus Stevens, and George W. Julian vigorously opposed any watering down of the original bill; a few radicals, including Julian and Stevens, wanted a provision confiscating rebel lands and distributing them among Union soldiers.[42] William D. "Pig-Iron" Kelley of Pennsylvania, in a long speech full of digressions, maintained that Congress should not only insist on the "punishment of the conspirators" but also demand "security for the future" against the rebels. "We are to shape the future," he announced. "We cannot escape the duty. And 'conciliation, compromise, and concession' are not the methods we are to use."[43]

The efforts of Kelley and other radicals in the House of Representatives to obtain a stronger reconstruction bill proved futile. After much debate on amendments in an unsuccessful attempt by Ashley to satisfy all political elements, the House on February, 22, 1865, tabled the measure by a vote of 80 to 65, with 37 members not voting. Democrats and conservative Unionists of the border states, who were wary of any congressional requirements for the restoration of the Southern states, voted solidly for tabling the measure; a few Republicans joined them.[44] The *Springfield (MA) Weekly Republican* reported, "Thus the president's reconstruction policy stands, and the readmission of the recovered states will be obstructed by no inflexible rule, but each case can be determined according to circumstances existing when it comes up."[45]

Meanwhile, efforts in the Senate in early 1865 to challenge or modify the president's reconstruction plan centered on the question of seating members elected by his Union governments in Louisiana and Arkansas. Lincoln saw no reason why Congress should refuse to seat the senators from these states. On January 9, Senator Trumbull, chairman of the Judiciary Committee that handled the credentials of the Louisiana claimants, met with Lincoln. Later in the day, he sent a note requesting the president to verify statements General Banks provided the committee strongly supporting the Union government in Louisiana.[46] The president immediately replied, "All the statements which lie within the range of my knowledge are strictly true." He also said that he "was anxious" to secure the restoration of Louisiana to the Union, asking, "Can Louisiana be brought into proper practical relations with the Union sooner, by *admitting* or by *rejecting* the proposed Senators?" Lincoln's answer obviously was the former. Yet, ever sensitive to charges of interference in legislative matters, he did not want Trumbull to think that he was "out of place" in lobbying for the recognition of the Louisiana government and the seating of its senators.[47]

Trumbull promised Lincoln that he would support the Louisiana Union government and its senators. Even so, the president recognized that radicals in his party, joined by Democrats at the other political extreme, would attempt to prevent the seating of any Southern senator or representative elected under his reconstruction plan, which thereby would block congressional recognition of the restored Lincoln governments in those states. Louisiana was the test case.

On February 18, Trumbull, acting for the Judiciary Committee, dutifully presented a joint resolution in the Senate declaring that the Union government of Louisiana, which had been organized on April 6, 1864, should be recognized as the legitimate government of the state. Accordingly, Trumbull said, it should be "entitled to the guarantees and all other rights" under the U.S. Constitution. This meant also that the state's representatives in Congress should be seated. The proposed joint resolution contained an important caveat: it would not be effective until the House of Representatives approved it.[48]

Complications immediately arose. On February 23, Charles Sumner introduced an inflammatory, one-paragraph substitute for Trumbull's joint resolution on Louisiana. The Massachusetts senator's brief substitute would require black suffrage and other equal rights before a state could be restored and its representatives seated in Congress. Two days later, a bruising debate occurred between Sumner and conservative Unionist Reverdy Johnson. The Maryland senator, who often crossed swords with Sumner in the Senate, vehemently denounced Sumner's contention that Congress had the right to dictate a voting requirement for a state. Other border state senators joined in the opposition to the Sumner substitute, which led to its defeat by a bipartisan vote of 8 to 20. The 8 senators supporting Sumner's substitute were a fair indication of the core radical strength in the Senate at this time.[49]

The Massachusetts senator, however, continued the fight for the inclusion of equal rights provisions in Trumbull's Louisiana resolution. Late on February 25, Sumner offered a comprehensive substitute for the resolution, a tactic that greatly exasperated Trumbull, who had scheduled the vote on it for that day. The Illinois senator lashed out at his fellow Republican for his "determination to browbeat the Senate on the part of a minority" by delaying the vote in hopes of persuading absent members to support his substitute. Trumbull asked, "Does he [Sumner] hold in his hand the Senate of the United States, that, in his omnipotence, he is to say when votes should be taken, and public matters should be passed? . . . The Senator from Massachusetts has fought [the measure] day after day to prevent it coming up; and when a majority of the Senate has overruled him time and again, and decided that it should come up, he stands here at half after ten o'clock on Saturday night making dilatory motions to prevent the action of the body." Sumner replied in kind by declaring, "The Senator from Illinois draws upon his imagination, which, on this occasion is peculiarly lively. I know not that anybody has undertaken to browbeat unless it be himself" on a question, Sumner said, that was the most important one that Congress had faced—the reconstruction issue and black rights in the South.[50]

Much to the glee of the few Democrats and border state conservatives still in the chamber, the dustup between Republican senators continued when James Doolittle backed Trumbull against Sumner. In the exchange, the Massachusetts radical reminded the Senate of Doolittle's earlier support for black colonization. "Anything for freedom is dangerous to the Senator from Wisconsin," Sumner charged, though Doolittle, like Lincoln, had favored only voluntary black resettlement, not mandatory emigration as the border state senators had demanded. Finally, about midnight on February 25, when nothing had been decided, the exhausted senators agreed to adjourn.[51] When the Senate reassembled, it was faced with important financial and other business to act on before the session ended on March 3. The senators on both sides of the aisle then agreed to postpone the issue of seating the Southern senators and, for that matter, any action on reconstruction. Most members of the Senate and the House probably assumed that until they reconvened in December, Lincoln would have a free hand on reconstruction.[52]

On March 4, 1865, Abraham Lincoln took the oath of office for another term as president and delivered his classic Second Inaugural Address. He ended his brief address with a stirring appeal directed at both Northerners and Southerners as the war ended: "With malice toward none; with charity for all; with firmness in the right, as God gives us to see the right, let us strive on to finish the work we are in; to bind up the nation's wounds; to care for him who shall have borne the battle, and for his widow, and his orphan—to do all which may achieve and cherish a just, and a lasting peace, among ourselves, and with all nations."[53]

On April 9, General Lee surrendered his army at Appomattox Court House to General Grant, and an even larger Confederate force was on the verge of capitulating to General Sherman in North Carolina. Public elation at the ending of the war and victory soon gave way to tragedy. Members of Congress as well as other Americans awoke on Saturday, April 15, to the horrible news that a diehard pro-Confederate actor had struck down "the good and gentle, as well as truly great man" who had led the Union to victory.[54] Congressmen, including those who had opposed Lincoln, were shocked that such a dastardly act could have happen to an American president. They were also deeply saddened by the assassination of a person whom they knew well and found to be honest and trustworthy, despite the tremendous pressures of the war on him. Ben Wade, Lincoln's most persistent radical critic, was appalled by the murder, but in an angry and revengeful mood toward the assassin and the South, he reportedly told the new president, Andrew Johnson, "I thank God you are here. Mr. Lincoln had too much of human kindness in him to deal with these infamous traitors, and I am glad that it has fallen into your hands to deal out justice to them."[55] Wade, as well as other radicals, would soon be disappointed in Johnson.

The Ohio senator would serve as a pallbearer at the president's funeral, along with several other members of Congress, including Senator Reverdy Johnson of Maryland, the leading conservative opponent of Lincoln in the Thirty-Eighth Congress. Charles Sumner and other Republican colleagues delivered heartfelt public eulogies to the fallen president. Probably wisely, in view of the inflamed climate of opinion after the assassination, Democratic and Copperhead opponents of Lincoln avoided public appearances during the national period of mourning. It was left to Republican senator James W. Grimes of Iowa, who once privately proclaimed the president's administration "a disgrace from the beginning," to render history's judgment on Lincoln in the political battles of the Civil War. The day after the president died, Grimes wrote, "Mr. Lincoln is to be hereafter regarded as a saint. All his foibles, and faults, and shortcomings, will be forgotten, and he will be looked upon as the Moses who led the nation through a four years' bloody war, and died in sight of peace."[56]

EPILOGUE

Speculation on what Lincoln might have done had he lived and faced the hard realities of Southern reconstruction and postwar financial issues has become a cottage industry among historians and others. It is safe to say that his relationship with Congress and the cooperation between the two branches of the government on important policies would have been a lot better than that of his successor, Andrew Johnson. The Tennessee Unionist lacked Lincoln's political skill and a commitment to protect the fruits of Union victory in the war, which included bona fide freedom for black people. Within a year, Johnson, ironically claiming that he was following Lincoln's reconstruction policy, had caused the Republican majority in Congress to unite to resist his ill-advised efforts to restore the Southern states to the Union. In 1866, the Republicans acted quickly to invalidate Johnson's reconstruction plan and initiate the Fourteenth Amendment to the Constitution. Then in 1867, over the president's veto, Congress enacted military reconstruction for the South.

Given Lincoln's fundamental conservatism and his desire to see the rebel states restored as soon as possible to their "proper practical relation with the Union,"[1] would he have supported the controversial Fourteenth Amendment and also military reconstruction? Would he have backed federal-mandated black suffrage for the Southern states, as required by Congress in the Military Reconstruction Acts of 1867 and later in the Fifteenth Amendment? In his last public address, on April 11, 1865, Lincoln announced in reference to Louisiana's reconstruction that he would have preferred that the state had conferred "the elective franchise . . . on the very intelligent [black people], and those who serve our cause as soldiers."[2]

Yet Lincoln in his April 11 address did not say that he would use presidential power to require black political rights, nor did he say that he would recommend it to Congress. Despite increased demands by radicals such as Sumner, a minority on the issue of black suffrage as the war ended, Lincoln had agreed with conservatives that voting and office-holding requirements resided with the states. After the surrender of the rebel armies, he would have found it difficult if not impossible to plead "military necessity" for imposing black political rights on the South, as he had done in justifying the Emancipation Proclamation. Perhaps he would have gone further than his April 11 address and insisted that the Union governments in the South extend rights to the former slaves and prohibit the early return of former rebel leaders to political power and seats in Congress. But he had not succeeded in persuading Louisiana (white) Unionists in 1864 to enfranchise certain classes of black males when they drew up their new state constitution or to politically proscribe former Confederates except for their unpardoned leaders.

Finally, even if Lincoln had lived and agreed to some adjustments in his lenient reconstruction policy for former rebels, would congressional Republicans still have initiated the Fourteenth Amendment, a constitutional change that, in retrospect, had radical implications for America as well as the South? It is unlikely that Lincoln would have done so, but we will never know.

ACKNOWLEDGMENTS

In all my research and writing, the staff of the D. H. Hill Library at North Carolina State University has provided prompt and valuable assistance. Friends, both in Raleigh and elsewhere, have encouraged and aided my work, including this book. Colleagues Joe Mobley, Alex De Grand, and John Riddle, all senior scholars in different fields, have broadened my view of Lincoln and the Civil War period by making useful comments and raising questions that I had failed properly to consider. I owe a debt of gratitude as well to former colleague John David Smith of the University of North Carolina at Charlotte for his generous help in my scholarly efforts. I am extremely appreciative of the opportunity that Sylvia Frank Rodrigue and Richard Etulain, editors of the Concise Lincoln Library, have given me to write two books in this distinguished series. I also thank Judy Verdich of Southern Illinois University Press for the helpful assistance that she has provided. In addition, I greatly appreciate the painstaking attention that Joyce Bond gave in copy editing the manuscript.

It is a cliché, but I could not have written this and other books without the marvelous support of my wife of fifty-five years and counting, Betty Glenn Harris.

NOTES

Introduction

1. Abraham Lincoln, "Manuscript Prepared for the Pittsburgh Speech," February 15, 1861, in *The Collected Works of Abraham Lincoln*, ed. Roy P. Basler (New Brunswick, NJ: Rutgers University Press, 1953), 4:214.
2. Francis Fessenden, *Life and Public Services of William Pitt Fessenden* (Boston: Houghton Mifflin and Co., 1907), 1:259–60.
3. *Congressional Globe*, 37th Congress, 2nd Session (January 22, 1862), 440.
4. Morton Keller, *Affairs of State: Public Life in Late Nineteenth Century America* (Cambridge: Harvard University Press, 1977), 22.
5. *Congressional Globe*, 37th Congress, 2nd Session (June 27, 1862), 2972.
6. Horace White, *The Life of Lyman Trumbull* (Boston: Houghton Mifflin and Co., 1913), 218.
7. Isaac Newton Arnold, *The Life of Abraham Lincoln* (Chicago: Jansen, McClurg & Co., 1885), 385–86n.
8. White, *Life of Lyman Trumbull*, 219.
9. David Donald, *Lincoln Reconsidered: Essays on the Civil War* (New York: Vintage Books, 1956), 126.
10. James A. Rawley, *The Politics of Union: Northern Politics during the Civil War* (Hinsdale, IL: Dryden Press, 1974), 2.
11. Conservative Republican senator Orville H. Browning recorded in his diary that all congressmen on a train with Fessenden, including two other New England Republican senators, concurred that Senator Sumner was "cowardly, mean, malignant, tyrannical, hypocritical, and cringing and toadyish." They clearly found it difficult to work with Sumner in the Senate. Entry for November 28, 1862, *The Diary of Orville Hickman Browning*, vol. 1, *1850–1864* (Springfield: Illinois State Historical Library, 1925), 588.
12. *Congressional Globe*, 37th Congress, 2nd Session (May 6, 1862), 1950.
13. For the thesis that Lincoln and the Republicans by design ushered in an all-powerful federal government, see Richard F. Bensel, *Yankee Leviathan: The Origins of Central State Authority in America* (Cambridge, UK: Cambridge University Press, 1990); and Thomas J. DiLorenzo, *The Real Lincoln: A New Look at Abraham Lincoln, His Agenda, and an Unnecessary War* (Roseville, CA: Forum Press, 2002).
14. Lincoln, "Annual Message to Congress," December 6, 1864, *Collected Works*, 8:152.

1. Secession and War

1. Lincoln to Lyman Trumbull, December 10, 17, 1860, *Collected Works*, 4:149–50, 153. See also Lincoln to William Kellogg, December 11, 1860, and Lincoln to Elihu B. Washburne, December 13, 1860, ibid., 4:150, 151.

2. Daniel W. Crofts, *Reluctant Confederates: Upper South Unionists in the Secession Crisis* (Chapel Hill: University of North Carolina Press, 1989), 236. Often forgotten in the history of the compromise movement during the winter of 1860–61 was Stephen A. Douglas's Senate speech on January 3 denouncing the secessionists as well as the Republicans and declaring that the only alternative to war was compromise on slavery. Douglas warned, "War is disunion, certain, inevitable, irrevocable disunion." Russell McClintock, *Lincoln and the Decision for War: The Northern Response to Secession* (Chapel Hill: University of North Carolina Press, 2008), 115–16.

3. Lincoln to William H. Seward, January 19, 1861, *Collected Works*, 4:176.

4. Fessenden, *Life of William Pitt Fessenden*, 1:121–22, 125.

5. Glyndon G. Van Deusen, *William Henry Seward* (New York: Oxford University Press, 1967), 245.

6. David M. Potter, *The Impending Crisis, 1848–1861*, completed and ed. Don E. Fehrenbacher (New York: Harper & Row, 1976), 550–51.

7. *Congressional Globe*, 36th Congress, 2nd Session (March 2, 1861), 1380–81, 1382.

8. Ibid., 1382–83; see also Richard H. Abbott, *Cobbler in Congress: The Life of Henry Wilson, 1812–1875* (Lexington: University Press of Kentucky, 1972), 112–13.

9. William C. Harris, *Lincoln's Rise to the Presidency* (Lawrence: University Press of Kansas, 2007), 293–94.

10. Lincoln, "First Inaugural Address—Final Text," March 4, 1861, *Collected Works*, 4:271.

11. *Congressional Globe*, 37th Congress, Special Session of the Senate (March 8, 1861), 1446; Fessenden, *Life of William Pitt Fessenden*, 1:127.

12. *Congressional Globe*, 37th Congress, Special Session of the Senate (March 28, 1861), 1519.

13. Lincoln, "Proclamation Calling Militia and Convening Congress," April 15, 1861, *Collected Works*, 4:331–33.

14. Lincoln, "Proclamation Calling for 42,034 Volunteers," May 3, 1861, *Collected Works*, 4:353–54. One year later, Lincoln reported to Congress that on April 20, 1861, he had directed the secretary of the treasury "to advance, without requiring security," $2 million to three New Yorkers in order to meet requisitions for the immediate support of the army and the navy. According to his statement, he had taken this extraordinary action after consulting with his "constitutional advisers" and

department heads. Lincoln, "To the Senate and House of Representatives," May 26, 1862, *Collected Works*, 5:241–42.

15. For an excellent recent history of wartime Washington, see Kenneth J. Winkle, *Lincoln's Citadel: The Civil War in Washington, DC* (New York: W. W. Norton & Company, 2013).

16. Entry for August 5, 1861, *Browning Diary*, 493.

17. Allan Nevins, *The War for the Union*, vol. 1, *The Improvised War, 1861–1862* (New York: Charles Scribner's Sons, 1959), 188.

18. Leonard P. Curry, *Blueprint for Modern America: Nonmilitary Legislation of the First Civil War Congress* (Nashville: Vanderbilt University Press, 1968), 24–29.

19. Lincoln, "Message to Congress in Special Session," July 4, 1861, *Collected Works*, 4:421–24. The session was misnamed by the editors. Although Lincoln called Congress into an extraordinary session, it actually was the first session of the Thirty-Seventh Congress.

20. Ibid., 4:424–26.

21. Ibid., 4:426, 428–29.

22. Ibid., 4:429–31.

23. Ibid., 4:432–35.

24. Entry for July 3, 1861, *Browning Diary*, 475.

25. James G. Randall, *Lincoln the President: Springfield to Gettysburg* (New York: Dodd, Mead, 1945), 1:381.

26. Douglas L. Wilson, *Lincoln's Sword: The Presidency and the Power of Words* (New York; Alfred A. Knopf, 2006), 104.

27. Lincoln, "Message to Congress in Special Session," July 4, 1861, *Collected Works*, 4:431–32.

28. *Congressional Globe*, 37th Congress, 1st Session (July 10, 1861), 40–44, 54.

29. Nevins, *War for the Union*, 1:184.

30. *Congressional Globe*, 37th Congress, 1st Session (July 15, 1861), 131.

31. Ibid. (July 16, 1861), 139–42.

32. Russell F. Weigley, *A Great Civil War: A Military and Political History, 1861–1865* (Bloomington: Indiana University Press, 2000), 57.

33. Nevins, *War for the Union*, 1:195–96; Charles A. Jellison, *Fessenden of Maine: Civil War Senator* (Syracuse, NY: Syracuse University Press, 1962), 134–35.

34. William C. Harris, *With Charity for All: Lincoln and the Restoration of the Union* (Lexington: University Press of Kentucky, 1997), 22–23.

35. *Congressional Globe*, 37th Congress, 1st Session (July 15, 1861), 120.

36. Ibid. (July 22, 1861), 218–19; James G. Blaine, *Twenty Years of Congress: From Lincoln to Garfield* (Norwich, CT: Henry Bill Publishing Company, 1884), 1:349.

37. *Congressional Globe*, 37th Congress, 1st Session (August 2, 1861), 411–12.

38. Ibid. (August 3, 1861), 430–31. See also Curry, *Blueprint for Modern America*, 75–77.

39. Michael Burlingame, *Abraham Lincoln: A Life* (Baltimore: Johns Hopkins University Press, 2008), 2:174; Blaine, *Twenty Years of Congress*, 1:343.

40. For the Crittenden Resolution and also Johnson's, which the Senate soon adopted, see Henry Steele Commager, ed., *Documents of American History* (New York: Appleton-Century-Crofts, 1968), 395–96.

41. *Congressional Globe*, 37th Congress, 1st Session (July 22, 1861), 222–23.

42. Ibid. (July 25, 1861), 258–59.

43. Ibid., 259.

44. Ibid.

45. Ibid., 265.

46. Orville H. Browning to Abraham Lincoln, September 17, 30, 1861, Papers of Abraham Lincoln, Manuscript Division, Library of Congress, Washington, DC (hereafter cited as Lincoln Papers). http://memory.loc.gov/ammen/alhtml/alhome.html/.

47. Jellison, *Fessenden of Maine*, 138–39.

48. Lyman Trumbull to "My Dear Sir," November 5, 1861, in White, *Life of Lyman Trumbull*, 171–72.

2. Congressional Activism

1. "The Tribune Almanac for 1862," *The Tribune Almanac for the Years 1838 to 1868, Inclusive* (New York: New York Tribune, 1868), 2:18–19. The political affiliation of the senators is based on my tally.

2. Lincoln, "Annual Message to Congress," December 3, 1861, *Collected Works*, 5:35–36.

3. Ibid., 5:39–40.

4. Ibid., 5:46.

5. *Congressional Globe*, 37th Congress, 2nd Session (May 8, 1862), 2014–16.

6. Ibid., 2017.

7. Lincoln, "Annual Message to Congress," December 3, 1861, *Collected Works*, 5:48.

8. Ibid.

9. Ibid., 5:48–49.

10. *Congressional Globe*, 37th Congress, 2nd Session (December 2, 1861), 5.

11. Ibid., 5–6.

12. Allen C. Guelzo, *Lincoln's Emancipation Proclamation: The End of Slavery in America* (New York: Simon & Schuster, 2004), 64–65.

13. David Donald, *Charles Sumner and the Rights of Man* (New York: Alfred A. Knopf, 1970), 54.

14. John Syrett, *The Civil War Confiscation Acts: Failing to Reconstruct the South* (New York: Fordham University Press, 2005), 21–22; *Congressional Globe*, 37th Congress, 2nd Session (December 5, 1861), 18–19.

15. *Congressional Globe*, 37th Congress, 2nd Session (March 4, 1862), 1049–50.

16. White, *Life of Lyman Trumbull*, 173–74.

17. Lincoln, "Message to Congress," March 6, 1862, *Collected Works*, 5:144–45.

18. Ibid., 5:145–46.

19. *New York Times*, March 8, 12, 1862; *New York Tribune*, March 7, 8, 11, 1862; *New York World*, March 7, 8, 1862.

20. Lincoln's meeting with the border state congressmen is based on a first-hand account by Representative James W. Crisfield of Maryland in Edward McPherson, *The Political History of the United States of America, during the Great Rebellion*, 2nd ed. (Washington, DC: Philp & Solomons, 1865), 210–11. For a fuller account of Lincoln's compensated emancipation proposal and its fate, see my *Lincoln and the Border States*, 165–82.

21. McPherson, *Political History*, 210.

22. Lincoln to Horace Greeley, March 24, 1862, *Collected Works*, 5:169.

23. *Congressional Globe*, 37th Congress, 2nd Session (March 12, 1862), 1191–92.

24. Ibid. (March 25, 1862), 1359.

25. Ibid. (March 12, 1862), 1191–92.

26. Ibid. (March 24, 25, 1862), 1133, 1358.

27. Ibid. (April 1, 1862), 1471–72.

28. Ibid. (April 3, 1862), 1526. Four of the Democrats voting against the district emancipation bill were from California and Oregon.

29. Ibid. (April 11, 1862), 1634–36, 1648.

30. Guelzo, *Lincoln's Emancipation Proclamation*, 86.

31. Lincoln, "Message to Congress," April 16, 1862, *Collected Works*, 5:192, 192n. The term "femes-covert" referred to dependent married women.

32. Lincoln, "Call for 300,000 Volunteers," July 1, 1862, *Collected Works*, 5:296–97, 297n.

33. Abbott, *Life of Henry Wilson*, 129; Guelzo, *Lincoln's Emancipation Proclamation*, 113.

34. Entry for July 1, 1862, *Browning Diary*, 555.

35. *Congressional Globe*, 37th Congress, 2nd Session (July 9, 1862), 3198.

36. Guelzo, *Lincoln's Emancipation Proclamation*, 113.

37. James W. Geary, *We Need Men: The Union Draft in the Civil War* (DeKalb: Northern Illinois University Press, 1991), 27.

38. Curry, *Blueprint for Modern America*, 88–89.

39. *Congressional Globe*, 37th Congress, 2nd Session (June 28, 1862), 2989–90.

40. Ibid., 2990, 2994.

41. Entry for July 1, 1862, *Browning Diary*, 555.

42. Curry, *Blueprint for Modern America*, 97–98; McPherson, *Political History*, 196–97.

43. Entry for July 14, 1862, *Browning Diary*, 558.

44. Lincoln, "To the Senate and House of Representatives," July 17, 1862, *Collected Works*, 5:328–31.

45. Syrett, *Civil War Confiscation Acts*, 55.

46. Lincoln, "Emancipation Proclamation—First Draft," [July 22, 1862], *Collected Works*, 5:336–37, 337n; Guelzo, *Lincoln's Emancipation Proclamation*, 121–23.

47. Lincoln, "Speech to Germans at Cincinnati, Ohio," February 12, 1861, *Collected Works*, 4:201.

48. *Congressional Globe*, 37th Congress, 2nd Session (February 28, 1862), 1031, 1035.

49. Curry, *Blueprint for Modern America*, 102–8; Phillip Shaw Paludan, *"A People's Contest": The Union and Civil War, 1861–1865* (New York: Harper & Row, 1988), 134–35.

50. Curry, *Blueprint for Modern America*, 116–18.

51. *Congressional Globe*, 37th Congress, 2nd Session (May 6, 1862), 1949–50.

52. Ibid., 1971.

53. Ibid. (June 20, 24, 1862), 2833–40, 2905–6. The Senate vote is on p. 2840.

54. James M. McPherson, *Ordeal by Fire: The Civil War and Reconstruction* (1982; repr., New York: McGraw-Hill, 2001), 405.

55. William Belmont Parker, *The Life and Public Services of Justin Smith Morrill* (Boston: Houghton Mifflin Company, 1924), 269–71.

56. *Congressional Globe*, 37th Congress, 2nd Session (May 19, June 10, 17, 1862), 2270, 2275, 2634.

3. A Time of Despair

1. Lincoln, "Preliminary Emancipation Proclamation," September 22, 1862, *Collected Works*, 5:336–37, 433–36.

2. Mark E. Neely Jr., *The Fate of Liberty: Abraham Lincoln and Civil Liberties* (New York: Oxford University Press, 1991), 52–53.

3. Lincoln, "Proclamation Suspending the Writ of Habeas Corpus," September 24, 1864, *Collected Works*, 5:436–37.

4. Entry for September 25, 1862, *The Civil War Diary of Gideon Welles: Lincoln's Secretary of the Navy*, ed. William E. Gienapp and Erica L. Gienapp (Urbana: University of Illinois Press, 2014), 59.

5. White, *Life of Lyman Trumbull*, 198–99.

6. Neely, *Fate of Liberty*, 68–72.
7. *Congressional Globe*, 37th Congress, 2nd Session (May 29, 1862), 2415, 2418–19.
8. Ibid.
9. Ibid. (July 16, 1862), 3320.
10. Ibid., 3397.
11. Entry for December 15, 1862, *Browning Diary*, 596.
12. Francis H. Pierpont to Abraham Lincoln, December 18, 1862; Pierpont et al. to Lincoln, December 20, 1862, Lincoln Papers.
13. Lincoln, "To Members of the Cabinet," December 23, 1862, *Collected Works*, 6:17.
14. The opinions of Stanton, Seward, and Blair, December 26, 1862; Bates, December 27, 1862; Chase and Welles, December 29, 1862, are in the Lincoln Papers.
15. John G. Nicolay and John Hay, *Abraham Lincoln: A History* (New York: Century Co., 1890), 6:312–13.
16. Bruce Tap, *Over Lincoln's Shoulder: The Committee on the Conduct of the War* (Lawrence: University Press of Kansas, 1998), 8, 166.
17. Fergus M. Bordewich, "The Radicals' War," *Civil War Monitor* 4 (Winter 2014): 45.
18. Ibid., 47; also, George W. Julian, *Political Recollections, 1840–1872* (1884; repr., Miami: Mnemosyne Publishing Co., 1883), 49–50.
19. Hans L. Trefousse, *The Radical Republicans: Lincoln's Vanguard for Racial Justice* (New York: Alfred A. Knopf, 1969), 246.
20. Ward Hill Lamon, *Recollections of Abraham Lincoln, 1847–1865* (Chicago: A. C. McClurg, 1895), 240–41.
21. Sister Mary Karl George, *Zachariah Chandler: A Political Biography* (East Lansing: Michigan State University Press, 1969), 77.
22. Bordewich, "Radicals' War," 47–48; George, *Zachariah Chandler*, 55–56.
23. Lincoln reportedly praised Porter for his generalship after the Battle of Antietam. Otto Eisenschiml, *The Celebrated Case of Fitz John Porter: An American Dreyfus Affair* (Indianapolis: Bobbs-Merrill Co., 1950), 68.
24. Ibid., 75.
25. James M. McPherson, *Crossroads of Freedom: Antietam* (New York: Oxford University Press, 2002), 53–54; Donald R. Jarman, *Fitz-John Porter, Scapegoat of Second Manassas: The Rise, Fall and Rise of the General Accused of Disobedience* (Jefferson, NC: McFarland & Co., 2009), 3.
26. William Marvel, *Lincoln's Autocrat: The Life of Edwin Stanton* (Chapel Hill: University of North Carolina Press, 2015), 271–72.
27. Robert J. Cook, *Civil War Senator: William Pitt Fessenden and the Fight to Save the American Republic* (Baton Rouge: Louisiana State University Press, 2001), 127.

28. See especially entries for December 16, 17, 18, 22, 1862, *Browning Diary*, 596–604.

29. The undated manuscript was printed in Fessenden, *Life of William Pitt Fessenden*, 1:236–40.

30. Ibid., 1:232.

31. Ibid., 1:232–33.

32. Ibid., 1:235–36.

33. Ibid., 1:236–38; entry for December 17, 1862, *Browning Diary*, 599.

34. Fessenden, *Life of William Pitt Fessenden*, 1:238. Collamer's paper is printed on pp. 239–40. The original, dated December 17, 1862, is found in the Lincoln Papers.

35. Entry for December 18, 1862, *Browning Diary*, 600.

36. Ibid., 600–601.

37. Fessenden, *Life of William Pitt Fessenden*, 1:240–42.

38. Ibid., 1:240–42.

39. Ibid., 1:242.

40. Entry for December 19, 1862, *Civil War Diary of Gideon Welles*, 100.

41. Ibid., 100–101; Fessenden, *Life of William Pitt Fessenden*, 1:243–44.

42. Fessenden, *Life of William Pitt Fessenden*, 1:244.

43. Ibid.; entry for December 19, 1862, *Civil War Diary of Gideon Welles*, 100.

44. Entry for December 19, 1862, *Civil War Diary of Gideon Welles*, 100–101.

45. Ibid., 101; Fessenden, *Life of William Pitt Fessenden*, 1:245.

46. Entry for December 22, 1862, *Browning Diary*, 603.

47. Entry for December 20, 1862, *Civil War Diary of Gideon Welles*, 104–5; entry for December 22, 1862, *Browning Diary*, 604.

48. Henry Dawes to Electra Dawes, February 12, 1863, Henry Dawes Papers, Manuscript Division, Library of Congress, Washington, DC.

49. Lincoln, "Annual Message to Congress," December 1, 1862, *Collected Works*, 5:518–19.

50. Ibid., 5:524–26.

51. Lincoln, "Annual Message to Congress," December 8, 1863, *Collected Works*, 7:47–48.

52. Lincoln, "Annual Message to Congress," December 1, 1862, *Collected Works*, 5:522–24.

53. Ibid., 5:527. The quotes are from Lincoln, "Preliminary Emancipation Proclamation," September 22, 1862, *Collected Works*, 5:434.

54. Lincoln, "Annual Message to Congress," December 1, 1862, *Collected Works*, 5:530.

55. Ibid., 5:531.

56. Ibid., 5:534–35.

57. Ibid., 5:537.

58. Entry for December 1, 1862, *Browning Diary*, 591.
59. *Liberator*, December 5, 12, 1862; Henry Winter Davis, *Speeches and Addresses Delivered in the Congress of the United States and on Several Public Occasions by Henry Winter Davis of Maryland* (New York: Harper & Brothers, 1867), 305–6.
60. McPherson, *Political History*, 224–26; *Congressional Globe*, 37th Congress, 3rd Session (February 12, 1863), 897–903.
61. Marvel, *Life of Edwin Stanton*, 274.
62. Eugene Converse Murdock, *Patriotism Limited, 1862–1865: The Civil War Draft and the Bounty System* (Kent, OH: Kent State University Press, 1967), 7.
63. *Congressional Globe*, 37th Congress, 3rd Session (February 24, 1863), 1263.
64. Ibid., 1256–57.
65. Ibid. (March 2, 1863), 1442–43.
66. Geary, *We Need Men*, 61.
67. Entry for February 1, 1863, *Browning Diary*, 622.
68. *Congressional Globe*, 37th Congress, 3rd Session (March 2, 1863), 445–48.

4. Union Resurgence

1. Lincoln to Erastus Corning and Others, [June 12, 1863], *Collected Works*, 6:265–66.
2. Mark E. Neely Jr., *Lincoln and the Triumph of the Nation: Constitutional Conflict in the American Civil War* (Chapel Hill: University of North Carolina Press, 2011), 86.
3. Geary, *We Need Men*, 154–55.
4. Lincoln, "To the Senate and House of Representatives," June 8, 1864, *Collected Works*, 7:380, 380n. For the statistics on conscription and those men who avoided the draft by paying commutation fees and also by hiring substitutes, compared with the total number of men who served in the Union army, see Weigley, *Great Civil War*, 236.
5. For the "Etheridge plot," see Herman Belz, *Reconstructing the Union: Theory and Policy during the Civil War* (Ithaca, NY: Cornell University Press, 1969), 151n.
6. "The Tribune Almanac for 1864," *The Tribune Almanac for the Years 1838 to 1868*, 2:24–25.
7. Entry for December (no date) 1863, *Civil War Diary of Gideon Welles*, 318.
8. Lincoln, "Annual Message to Congress," December 8, 1863, *Collected Works*, 7:36.
9. Ibid., 7:41–42.
10. Ibid., 7:42–44, 46–47.

11. Ibid., 7:47–48.
12. Ibid., 7:49.
13. Ibid., 7:49–50.
14. Ibid., 7:50–51; Lincoln, "Proclamation of Amnesty and Reconstruction," December 8, 1863, *Collected Works*, 7:53–56.
15. Lincoln, "Proclamation of Amnesty and Reconstruction," December 8, 1863, *Collected Works*, 8:53–56.
16. Lincoln, "Annual Message to Congress," December 8, 1863, *Collected Works*, 7:52. See John C. Rodrigue, *Lincoln and Reconstruction* (Carbondale: Southern Illinois University Press, 2013), for an excellent, updated account of Lincoln's reconstruction plan.
17. Entry for [December 9, 1863], *Inside Lincoln's White House: The Complete Civil War Diary of John Hay*, ed. Michael Burlingame and John R. Turner Ettlinger (Carbondale: Southern Illinois University Press, 1997), 121–22.
18. Ibid., 122.
19. *New York Tribune*, December 11, 1863; *Chicago Tribune*, December 10, 1863; *National Anti-Slavery Standard*, December 19, 1863; entry for December 11, 1863, *The Diary of George Templeton Strong*, ed. Allan Nevins and Milton Halsey Thomas (New York: Macmillan, 1952), 3:379.
20. Cook, *Civil War Senator*, 161.
21. Hans L. Trefousse, *Thaddeus Stevens: Nineteenth-Century Egalitarian* (Chapel Hill: University of North Carolina Press, 1997), 138; William B. Hesseltine, *Lincoln's Plan of Reconstruction* (1960; repr., Gloucester, MA: Peter Smith, 1963), 100.
22. As reported in the *New York Tribune*, December 11, 1863.
23. Harris, *With Charity for All*, 138, 300n51.
24. *Speech of Hon. Reverdy Johnson, of Maryland, Delivered before the Brooklyn McClellan Central Association, October 21, 1864* (Brooklyn: Brooklyn McClellan Association, 1864), 8–9, 12–13.
25. *Richmond Sentinel*, December 14, 1863.
26. *Congressional Globe*, 39th Congress, 1st Session (December 21, 1863), 70.
27. Belz, *Reconstructing the Union*, 183–85, 185n; Harris, *With Charity for All*, 142.
28. David Herbert Donald, Jean Harvey Baker, and Michael Holt, *The Civil War and Reconstruction* (New York: W. W. Norton & Co., 2001), 305–7.
29. Allan Nevins, *The War for the Union*, vol. 3, *The Organized War, 1863–1864* (New York: Charles Scribner's Sons, 1970), 91; Blaine, *Twenty Years of Congress*, 1:507–9; Trefousse, *Thaddeus Stevens*, 143–44.

30. *Congressional Globe*, 38th Congress, 1st Session (February 15, 1864), 659; William E. Parrish, *A History of Missouri*, vol. 3, *1860 to 1875* (Columbia: University of Missouri Press, 1973), 92.

31. *Congressional Globe*, 38th Congress, 1st Session (February 15, 1864), 660. For Trumbull's role in Congress's consideration of the proposed antislavery amendment, see Mark M. Krug, *Lyman Trumbull: Conservative Radical* (New York: A. S. Barnes and Co., 1965), 217–20.

32. Blaine, *Twenty Years of Congress*, 1:504.

33. Krug, *Lyman Trumbull*, 218–19; *Congressional Globe*, 38th Congress, 1st Session (March 28, 1864), 1317–18.

34. Krug, *Lyman Trumbull*, 219.

35. *Congressional Globe*, 38th Congress, 1st Session (March 28, 1864), 1319–24.

36. Ibid. (April 5, 1864), 1419–24; White, *Life of Lyman Trumbull*, 227. Johnson's speech, which differs slightly from the account in the *Congressional Globe*, was also issued as a pamphlet. *Speech of Hon. Reverdy Johnson, of Maryland, in Support of the Resolution to Amend the Constitution so as to Abolish Slavery, Delivered in the Senate of the United States, April 5, 1864* (Washington, DC, 1864).

37. *Congressional Globe*, 38th Congress, 1st Session (April 8, 1864), 1490.

38. Ibid. (June 15, 1864), 2989.

39. Blaine, *Twenty Years of Congress*, 1:506.

40. Michael Vorenberg, *Final Freedom: The Civil War, the Abolition of Slavery, and the Thirteenth Amendment* (Cambridge, UK: Cambridge University Press, 2001), 137–38.

41. Ibid., 137; Blaine, *Twenty Years of Congress*, 1:506–7.

42. *Congressional Globe*, 38th Congress, 1st Session (June 15, 1864), 2995.

43. Quoted in Vorenberg, *Final Freedom*, 139.

44. McPherson, *Political History*, 410, 413.

45. James A. Rawley, *Edwin D. Morgan, 1811–1893: Merchant in Politics* (New York: Columbia University Press 1955), 198–99; Richard N. Current, *The Lincoln Nobody Knows* (New York: Hill and Wang, 1958), 229.

46. George W. Julian, *Political Recollections, 1840–1872* (Chicago: Jansen, McClung & Company, 1884), 243–44.

47. Gerald S. Henig, *Henry Winter Davis: Antebellum and Civil War Congressman from Maryland* (New York: Twayne Publishers, 1973), 196–97.

48. Julian, *Political Recollections*, 246.

49. Henig, *Henry Winter Davis*, 205–7; Belz, *Reconstructing the Union*, 210.

50. Belz, *Reconstructing the Union*, 210–11.

51. *Congressional Globe*, 38th Congress, 1st Session (May 4, 1864), 2107–8.

52. Harold M. Hyman, ed., *The Radical Republicans and Reconstruction, 1861–1870* (Indianapolis: Bobbs-Merrill, 1967), 128–34.

53. *Congressional Globe*, 38th Congress, 1st Session (May 4, 1864), 2108.
54. Belz, *Reconstructing the Union*, 213.
55. *Congressional Globe*, 38th Congress, 1st Session (July 1, 1864), 3449.
56. Ibid., 3450–51.
57. Entry for July 4, 1864, *Inside Lincoln's White House*, 218.
58. Ibid., 218. Hay, a Lincoln secretary, was apparently in the room and heard the Lincoln-Chandler exchange.
59. Entry for July 4, 1864, *Inside Lincoln's White House*, 218.
60. Ibid., 218–19.
61. Lincoln, "Proclamation Concerning Reconstruction," July 8, 1864, *Collected Works*, 7:433–34.
62. Quoted in Henig, *Henry Winter Davis*, 212.
63. Blaine, *Twenty Years of Congress*, 2:43.
64. Trefousse, *Thaddeus Stevens*, 147.
65. The Wade-Davis Manifesto can be found in Hyman, ed., *Radical Republicans and Reconstruction*, 137–47.
66. Ibid.
67. Blaine, *Twenty Years of Congress*, 2:43.
68. Henig, *Henry Winter Davis*, 216–17, quoting the *Chicago Tribune*, August 11, 1864, and the *New York Times*, August 9, 1864.
69. Entries for August 6, 8, 1864, *Civil War Diary of Gideon Welles*, 464, 466–67.
70. Henig, *Henry Winter Davis*, 221; Hans L. Trefousse, *Benjamin Franklin Wade: Radical Republican from Ohio* (New York: Twayne Publishers, 1963), 227.

5. Triumph and Tragedy

1. George, *Zachariah Chandler*, 114.
2. John Waugh, *Reelecting Lincoln: The Battle for the 1864 Presidency* (New York: Crown, 1997), 308.
3. Trefousse, *Thaddeus Stevens*, 148.
4. Entry for February 12, 1865, "George W. Julian Journal—Assassination of Lincoln," *Indiana Magazine of History* 11 (1915): 328.
5. Lincoln, "Annual Message to Congress," December 6, 1864, *Collected Works*, 8:149.
6. Ibid., 8:151.
7. Ibid., 8:140–41.
8. Ibid., 8:137.
9. Cook, *Civil War Senator*, 172–73.
10. Lincoln, "Annual Message to Congress," December 6, 1864, *Collected Works*, 8:143–44.
11. Ibid., 8:146–47.

12. *Congressional Globe*, 38th Congress, 2nd Session (January 9, 1865), 158.
13. Ibid. (January 13, 1865), 250–51.
14. David A. Nichols, *Lincoln and the Indians: Civil War Policy* (St. Paul: Minnesota Historical Society Press, 1978), 210; William C. Harris, *Lincoln's Last Months* (Cambridge: Belknap Press of Harvard University Press, 2004), 173.
15. Lincoln, "Annual Message to Congress," December 6, 1864, *Collected Works*, 8:152.
16. *Congressional Globe*, 38th Congress, 2nd Session (January 5, 1865), 124.
17. Ibid. (December 14, 1864), 38–42. The quote is on p. 38.
18. For the documents relating to the Davis resolution, see McPherson, *Political History*, 349–54.
19. *Congressional Globe*, 38th Congress, 2nd Session (December 15, 1864), 48.
20. "Joint Resolution on Mexican Affairs" in Davis, *Speeches and Addresses*, 456–57, 474.
21. Entry for December 15, 1864, *Civil War Diary of Gideon Welles*, 548.
22. See McPherson, *Political History*, 600.
23. Harris, *Lincoln's Last Months*, 166.
24. *New York Times*, December 20, 1864.
25. *Congressional Globe*, 38th Congress, 2nd Session (January 6, 1865), 138.
26. Charles M. Segal, ed., *Conversations with Lincoln* (New York: Putnam, 1961), 362–63.
27. *Congressional Globe*, 38th Congress, 2nd Session (January 13, 1865), 258–63.
28. For an account of the Blair mission, see my article "The Hampton Roads Peace Conference: A Final Test of Lincoln's Presidential Leadership," *Journal of the Abraham Lincoln Association* 21 (Winter 2000): 34–37. The italics are mine.
29. James M. Ashley to Abraham Lincoln, January 31, 1865; Lincoln to Ashley, January 31, 1865, *Collected Works*, 8:248, 248n.
30. Harris, "Hampton Roads Peace Conference," 44–47, 55.
31. George, *Zachariah Chandler*, 120–21.
32. *Congressional Globe*, 38th Congress, 2nd Session (January 30, 1865), 495–96.
33. Schuyler Colfax to Abraham Lincoln, February 8, 1865, Lincoln Papers.
34. *Congressional Globe*, 38th Congress, 2nd Session (February 8, 1865), 657–60.
35. Noah Brooks, *Washington in Lincoln's Time* (New York: Rinehart, 1958), 206–7.
36. *Congressional Globe*, 38th Congress, 2nd Session (February 10, 1865), 733.

37. Ibid., 730–31, 733, 738.
38. For the provisions of the Ashley bill, see McPherson, *Political History*, 576.
39. Printed copy of a bill to guarantee to certain states whose governments have been usurped or overthrown a republican form of government, December 15, 1864, in Lincoln Papers. Professor Herman Belz, author of the standard account of the debate on wartime reconstruction, concludes that Lincoln's emendations on the document indicated his willingness to support the Ashley bill. Belz, *Reconstructing the Union*, 90, 252.
40. Entry for December 18, 1864, *Inside Lincoln's White House*, 253.
41. Ibid.
42. George W. Julian, *Speeches on Political Questions* (New York: Hurd and Houghton, 1872), 212–13.
43. *Congressional Globe*, 38th Congress, 2nd Session (January 16, 1865), 281, 290.
44. Ibid. (February 22, 1865), 1002–3.
45. *Springfield (MA) Weekly Republican*, February 25, 1865, quoted in Belz, *Reconstructing the Union*, 267.
46. Lyman Trumbull to Abraham Lincoln, January 9, 1865, Lincoln Papers.
47. Lincoln to Lyman Trumbull, January 9, 1865, *Collected Works*, 8:207.
48. McPherson, *Political History*, 579–80.
49. Ibid., 580; *Congressional Globe*, 38th Congress, 2nd Session (February 25, 1865), 1095–99.
50. *Congressional Globe*, 38th Congress, 2nd Session (February 25, 1865), 1095–99.
51. Ibid., 1110–11.
52. Harris, *With Charity for All*, 245.
53. Lincoln, "Second Inaugural Address," March 4, 1865, *Collected Works*, 8:332–33.
54. Entry for April 14, 1865, *Civil War Diary of Gideon Welles*, 624.
55. Thomas R. Turner, *The Assassination of Abraham Lincoln* (Malabar, FL: Krieger Publishing Co., 1999), 61.
56. Joshua Zeitz, "The Assassination of Abraham Lincoln: The History of How We Came to Revere Abraham Lincoln," *Smithsonian Magazine* (February 2014); James W. Grimes to his wife, April 16, 1865, in William Salter, *The Life of James W. Grimes* (New York: Appleton, 1876), 278.

Epilogue

1. Lincoln, "Last Public Address," April 11, 1865, *Collected Works*, 8:403.
2. Ibid.

ESSAY ON SOURCES

No effort has been made to mention all the sources for the book in this essay. Full citations of the materials are given in the notes section.

By far the most important contemporary sources for research on Lincoln and Congress for this book were *The Collected Works of Abraham Lincoln* (1953–55, 1974, 1990) and the *Congressional Globe* for 1861–65. Although not free of error, the *Globe* proved indispensable for the proceedings and speeches in Congress. Another useful source was the Papers of Abraham Lincoln in the Library of Congress. *The Diary of Orville Hickman Browning*, vol. 1, *1850–1864* (1925) was essential for the first two years of the war, when Browning was in the Senate and often met with Lincoln. Recently published, *The Civil War Diary of Gideon Welles: Lincoln's Secretary of the Navy* (2014) provided useful information and comments by Lincoln's acerbic secretary of the navy on the president's relationship with Congress and individual members. Likewise, *Inside Lincoln's White House: The Complete Civil War Diary of John Hay* (1997) was an important source of information from the perspective of the president and his secretary.

Various congressional resolutions, bills, roll calls, and other materials are found in *The Political History of the United States of America, during the Great Rebellion* (1865), edited by Edward McPherson, who was the clerk of the House of Representatives during the latter part of the war. A valuable source, especially on the Senate effort to reshape the president's cabinet, was the two-volume *Life and Public Services of William Pitt Fessenden* (1907), by Francis Fessenden. Although all were partisan, major newspapers provided some useful information and opinions on Congress and the president. These included the *New York Tribune, New York Times, New York Herald, New York World*, and *Chicago Tribune*.

The Civil War era was an age of pamphlets, and several of the speeches in Congress and in political campaigns are available for research in their digital editions. Biographies of the main congressional leaders, which are cited in the endnotes, contain not only valuable information and analysis but also correspondence and documents that cannot be found elsewhere. In addition, biographies of Lincoln were consulted, including David Donald's *Lincoln* (1995), which is generally regarded as the most authoritative one-volume biography of the sixteenth president, and Michael Burlingame's magisterial and indispensable two-volume *Abraham Lincoln: A Life* (2008).

Specialized scholarly works offered considerable information and insights for this study. On civil liberties, Mark Neely Jr.'s *The Fate of Liberty: Abraham Lincoln and Civil Liberties* (1991) was the best source on the issue of the government's suppression of dissent during the war. The tension between the administration, including the military, and Congress over congressional authority to investigate and seek changes in the prosecution of the war has been ably told in Bruce Tap's *Over Lincoln's Shoulder: The Committee on the Conduct of the War* (1998). James W. Geary's penetrating work, *We Need Men: The Union Draft in the Civil War* (1991), was the best study on this highly controversial subject. The debate in Congress over the seizure of rebel property and Lincoln's reservations regarding its constitutional justification are illuminated in John Syrett, *The Civil War Confiscation Acts: Failing to Reconstruct the South* (2005). The debate in Congress over emancipation and Lincoln's decision to issue his antislavery proclamation have been well described and analyzed by Allen C. Guelzo in *Lincoln's Emancipation Proclamation: The End of Slavery in America* (2004). Michael Vorenberg's *Final Freedom: The Civil War, the Abolition of Slavery, and the Thirteenth Amendment* (2001) completed the story on the ending of slavery.

No account that focused on Congress was more important in the research for this book than Leonard P. Curry, *Blueprint for Modern America: Nonmilitary Legislation of the First Civil War Congress* (1968). Unfortunately, Professor Curry did not continue his study with a book on the second Civil War Congress, 1863–65. Allan G. Bogue's *The Earnest Men: Republicans of the Civil War Senate* (1981) provided an interesting quantitative analysis of the voting patterns in the Senate during the war. Hans L. Trefousse's *The Radical Republicans: Lincoln's Vanguard for Racial Justice* (1969) was helpful in understanding the position of radicals in Congress. Also informative for the last part of the war was Michael Les Benedict, *A Compromise of Principle: Congressional Republicans and Reconstruction* (1974). On the debates over reconstruction, Herman Belz's *Reconstructing the Union: Theory and Policy during the Civil War* (1969) was essential, though this book differs with him on some issues. In addition, my book *With Charity for All: Lincoln and the Restoration of the Union* (1997) and also John C. Rodrigue's *Lincoln and Reconstruction* (2013) were consulted for important insights.

General histories of the Civil War proved important for specific information and understanding of the issues and the context in which Lincoln and Congress worked. The following works were the most useful on the war: Russell F. Weigley, *A Great Civil War: A Military and Political History, 1861–1865* (2000); James M. McPherson, *Battle Cry of Freedom: The Civil War Era* (1988); two volumes of Allan Nevins's *The War for the Union*, vol. 1, *The Improvised War, 1861–1862* (1959), and vol. 3, *The Organized War, 1863–1864* (1970); and Phillip Shaw Paludan's *"A People's Contest": The Union and Civil War, 1861–1865* (1988).

INDEX

Italicized page numbers followed
by "*g*" indicate gallery photographs.

William C. Harris, a professor emeritus of history at North Carolina State University, is the author or editor of twelve books on such topics as Lincoln, the Civil War, and reconstruction. His book *Lincoln and the Border States: Preserving the Union* was a cowinner of the 2012 Lincoln Prize.

**CONCISE
LINCOLN
LIBRARY**

This series of concise books fills a need for short studies of the life, times, and legacy of President Abraham Lincoln. Each book gives readers the opportunity to quickly achieve basic knowledge of a Lincoln-related topic. These books bring fresh perspectives to well-known topics, investigate previously overlooked subjects, and explore in greater depth topics that have not yet received book-length treatment. For a complete list of current and forthcoming titles, see www.conciselincolnlibrary.com.

Other Books in the Concise Lincoln Library